After the /Xam Bushmen

Song of the Broken String

Poems From A Lost Oral Tradition

by

Stephen Watson

Sheep Meadow Press
Riverdale-on-Hudson, New York

For my Parents,
Bob and Iris Watson

A CIP cataloging record of this book is available from the Library of Congress. ISBN 1-878818-43-0. Printed on acid-free paper in the United States. This book meets the guidelines for permanence and durability of the Committee on Production Guidelines for Book Longevity of the Council on Library Resources.

Acknowledgements

Versions of most of these poems, including an earlier, shorter version of my Introduction, first appeared in *Sound from the Thinking Strings*, edited by Pippa Skotnes, a limited edition published by her own Axeage Private Press in 1991. It was at her suggestion that I began work on these translations and I wish to record, first and foremost, my gratitude to her for introducing me to the world of the /Xam.

The work itself could never have proceeded without the information I was able to glean from the work of several scholars. In particular, I should like to mention Roger L. Hewitt, Mathias Guenther, and Patricia Vinnicombe. The books of Hewitt and Guenther were especially useful; in fact, they became my indispensable guides.

During the period I worked on these translations, I was fortunate to receive much helpful comment from several friends: Patrick Cullinan, Michael King, Douglas Reid Skinner, Mike Nicol, Peter Sacks, Robert Berold, Rodney Constantine, and Hugh Corder. I am indebted to all of them, but most of all to Sandra Dodson.

Several of these poems have also been published in *The Colorado Review, New Coin, New Contrast, Origini*, and *Partisan Review*.

The Publisher would like to thank the father and son team of Anthony and Geoffrey O'Brien for suggesting we publish this book.

—S.M.

Cover Illustration: Odilon Redon drawing from the Woodner Family Collection.

Contents

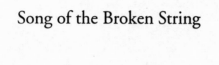

Song of the Broken String

Introduction

I

The versions that appear in this book would not have been possible without five people whose lives briefly converged in the Cape Colony over a century ago. Had it not been for a German linguist, W. H. Bleek, and his sister-in-law, Lucy Lloyd, the oral records which now bear their respective names, and which my versions use as their point of departure, would never have been collected. Without three nineteenth-century Bushmen and their extraordinary gifts as storytellers, what these records preserve—the oral traditions of the oldest of all South African cultures—would have been lost forever. If this book is indebted to anyone, it is chiefly to these five people.

Dr. Bleek first came to southern Africa in the 1850s, employed by Bishop Colenso in Natal to produce a work on the Zulu language. Later, he settled in Cape Town. In the late 1860s it came to his attention that a number of /Xam were working as convicts on the construction of the new breakwater in Cape Town's harbor. Most of them had been brought there from the northern Cape to serve out sentences of hard labor for crimes like stock theft. Aware (as few others were at the time) that these convicts belonged to a people whose culture was unlikely to survive for much longer, Bleek prevailed upon the then governor of the Colony, Sir Philip Wodehouse, to have several /Xam passed into his service. He devoted the last five years of his life to interviewing these people, first learning their language and then devising a phonetic script for its notation. With the assistance of Lucy Lloyd, who did most of the transcribing, he was thus able to preserve some of the folklore, songs, and other stories that formed part of their oral tradition. Out of these farsighted, painstaking labors came the 138 notebooks, amounting to more than twelve thousand pages, that comprise the Bleek and Lloyd collection, presently housed in the archives of the University of Cape Town.

It is one of the world's most remarkable ethnographic records. No less extraordinary must have been the circumstances in which it was put together. We know, for instance, that the /Xam informants lived in grass huts at the bottom of the garden of Bleek's home in Mowbray, Cape Town. Dislocating as these circumstances must have been, the actual conditions in which they narrated must have made matters even more difficult. Oral literature is inseparable from its performance and the context of such performance. Not to have had their own people as audience must have made the work of narration that much more artificial for them, not to say bizarre. We have to imagine Bleek and Lloyd's individual informants sitting across a table from them, having to break the flow of their narratives so that each sentence might be written down. We may imagine the incessant work of explication necessary before Bleek or Lloyd could supply the literal, word-for-word English translation that accompanies the phonetic script, which I have used for my own "double translations." And we may further appreciate the difficulties involved if we visualize for a moment what it must be like to be similarly placed, required to explain to a complete foreigner what our culture today means by the doctrine of some such thing as the Holy Trinity.

Bleek and Lloyd were fortunate, however, in finding outstanding narrators in the three men known as //Kabbo, /Han≠kasso, and Dia!kwain. All my versions in this book are based on their testimony. Both //Kabbo and /Han≠kasso, who were related by marriage, came from the same region of the north-western Cape, near present-day Kenhardt; Dia!kwain had his home in the Katkop area, some hundred miles to the west. All were members of what is usually called the /Xam, a word which denotes one of the several Bushman linguistic groups. No doubt there was once a time when bands of such people, speaking the same click language, were spread throughout the Cape. But by the time Bleek and Lloyd embarked upon their work in the early 1870s, the /Xam were largely confined to the area south of the Orange River, a region which was one of the last areas in the country to be settled by European farmers. Given its aridity and remoteness from major centers, it was also their final place of refuge, the one place left in the Colony where they could more or less follow the lives of hunters and gatherers.

Yet even then, in the second half of the nineteenth century, that way of life was under attack. This is reflected, not least, in those personal names which suggest some degree of acculturation. //Kabbo, for instance, was known by the alternative "Jantje Toorn"; /Han≠kasso, his son-in-law, as "Klein Jantje." Moreover, most of the informants, like the scores of other /Xam sent to Cape Town to work on the breakwater, were sentenced for crimes which must have been provoked by the invasion of white settlers into their world. Neither //Kabbo nor Dia!kwain would ever have been arrested for sheep stealing or murdering a white farmer had not their patterns of hunting and gathering already been violently disrupted, their lands threatened by enclosure, their traditional sources of food increasingly jeopardized. In fact, by the 1850s, many of the /Xam were already familiar with another pattern of life–that of bonded servants and laborers on white-owned farms. They were no longer able to be the wholly stone age people their ancestors had been. Most of them had become, in the words of Bleek's daughter, Dorothea, "Colonial Bushmen."

We know all too little about the informants themselves. Among other odds and ends, Bleek notes that //Kabbo was about sixty years of age and that he was a particularly skilled narrator: he "patiently watched until a sentence had been written down, before proceeding with what he was telling." His name meant "Dream," and although his prison record states that he had "no religion," there is reason to believe that he was a medicine man, able to control rain. Dia!kwain, according to Dorothea Bleek, was known as her father's "pet murderer," in reality "a soft-hearted mortal" who had allegedly shot one Jacob Kruger after the latter had threatened to kill him and his family. But all such biographical details seem incidental when set beside what these men achieved as narrators. If it is now widely recognized that Bushman rock art possesses, in its finest examples, a power and complexity easily the equal of the great touchstones of painting elsewhere in the world, then it is chiefly through //Kabbo, Dia!kwain and /Han≠kasso that we have evidence for what this magnificent tradition of painting might lead us to assume: an equivalent power, equal depth and corresponding beauty in their oral traditions.

W. H. Bleek died prematurely in 1875, having suffered prolonged ill-health. //Kabbo, though able to leave Cape Town and return to his place hundreds of miles to the north, was to die little more than a year later. As far as is known, Dia!kwain left the Bleek household in 1876 and subsequently spent several months working for a doctor in Calvinia. One day he set off to visit his sister and never returned. Legend has it that he was murdered by some farmers in retaliation for his earlier crime. /Han≠kasso, too, rapidly drops from sight. Although some of their stories would survive them, particularly in the selection entitled *Specimens of Bushmen Folklore* which Lucy Lloyd finally managed to publish in 1911, not long before her own death, the matrix out of which they came, a culture in continuous existence for something like five thousand years, was soon to follow them into oblivion.

II

As early as 1655, only three years after the Dutch East Company had established a supply station at the Cape, J. Wintervogel was to make the first recorded mention of the Bushmen, describing them as "a certain tribe, very low in stature, and very lean, entirely savage, without any huts, cattle, or anything in the world, clad in little skins." In one very real sense, the end of the Bushmen was already prefigured in words like these. For they are entirely characteristic of the dominant way in which these people were perceived, almost from the very outset, by the initial white colonists in South Africa.

In the two subsequent centuries the denigration scarcely veiled in Wintervogel's words would be ritually, thoughtlessly, endorsed by others. As late as 1874, *The Times* could carry a report which, referring to a Bushman exhibition in London, exuded all the self-confidence of the bigot: "In appearance they are little above the monkey tribe. They are continually crouching, warming themselves by the fire, chatting or growling, smoking etc. They are sullen, silent and savage—mere animals in propensity, and worse than animals in appearance." Other nineteenth-century European observers went still further in denying the Bushmen any possible membership in the human family, referring to them as "this ugliest specimen of the human race," their offspring "absolutely repulsive," like "yellow toads of larger size than usual," their "mien and gestures" displaying "the true physiognomy of the small blue ape of Kaffaria."

Obviously, a race of people characterized in these sub-human terms would seem, almost by definition, to invite its own extermination. But, in reality, most instances of European prejudice towards the Bushmen were more the consequence than the cause of an historical process that was set in motion not long after the arrival of European colonists at the Cape in the middle of the seventeenth century. In the 2000 years before that, a people like the /Xam had doubtless been involved in skirmishes with neighboring Khoi (or "Hottentot") tribes as well as other black settlers moving into the Africa south of the Limpopo River. But the scale of these conflicts now seems relatively insignificant when set beside the catastrophic collision that ensued once the white settlers started trekking into the Cape interior, the ancestral home of the /Xam. This expansion, gathering momentum after the 1740s, was to initiate a state of almost permanent war between white colonist and Bushman, one which was to last for more than a hundred years. It is at once the most poorly documented as well as the most shameful episode in South Africa's entire history.

All the evidence suggests that it was also inevitable. "Our people coveted the land," one nineteenth-century white farmer was candid in declaring. Hungry for additional grazing for their cattle and livestock, it was only a matter of time before the nomadic white pastoralists, generally known as trekboers, moved northwards from Cape Town, pushing in increasing numbers into that area of low rainfall which is the Cape hinterland. As these people, expert with gun and horse, advanced, they decimated the herds of wild game on which the /Xam depended for their very survival. At the same time, the trekboers' herds ravaged the veld, reducing the seeds and roots which provided the Bushmen with their only other source of food. To make matters worse, the trekboers, unlike these indigenous people, would not countenance any notion of a communal sharing of the land; they simply confiscated the territory across which their livestock migrated in search of pasture. All too soon the contest for the possession of always scarce natural resources grew murderous. Faced more and more often with the prospect of starvation, the /Xam had no choice but to retaliate by preying on the herds of the whites. The latter responded more or less in kind, mounting commandos against the Bushmen groups, hunting them down as if the latter were worse than any beast of prey, initiating a cycle of violence and counter-violence that soon assumed the proportions of a "total war."

From the outset it was clear that the conflict could only be an unequal one: the colonists were mounted and armed with muskets while the /Xam's principal weapon was the bow and arrow. It was also a conflict made more barbaric by the especial character of those trek-boers who moved into the northwestern areas of the Cape. Described by a later historian as "the most primitive of the Colony's white inhabitants, almost entirely out of touch with the institutions of civilized society," these were a people who had every opportunity to operate way beyond the control of the colonial government in Cape Town. By all accounts, they wasted no opportunity to take the law into their own hands. Already, in 1785, a European visitor to the Cape could write: "Does a colonist at any time get sight of a Boshiesman, he takes fire immediately and spirits up his horse and dogs, in order to hunt him with more ardor and fury than he would a wild beast." In the subsequent century there would even be reports of white farmers going out to shoot Bushman parties "for the fun of the thing." There was indeed seldom any limit to the treachery and mercilessness of the white colonists in their war against the /Xam. The following eye-witness account of a massacre is representative of many, even in its bluntness:

> They surrounded the place during the night, spying the Bushmen's fires. At daybreak the firing commenced, and it lasted until the sun was up a little. The commando party loaded and fired, and re-loaded. A great many people (women and children) were killed that day. The men were absent. Only a few little children escaped, and they were distributed amongst the people composing the

commando. The women threw up their arms, crying for mercy, but no mercy was shown them. Great sin was perpetrated that day. I was taken by my master to hold his horses. I did not join in the shooting. I had no gun.

In point of fact, many adult /Xam, men and women, were never allowed the option of surrendering. If taken alive, they would be executed almost immediately. In part, this was sheer inhumanity and bloodlust. But, as hunters and gatherers, Bushmen and women also had no role to play in the particular economy of the trekboers. Should they be captured and forced to labor as the colonists' shepherds, the /Xam would lose no opportunity to abscond and re-join their own people. Their children, however, could be reduced more easily to the condition of "apprentices"—the expression current at the time for what we today would call slavery or enslavement.

Not surprisingly, the /Xam and other Bushmen groups developed their own stratagems to counter the colonists, bitterly resisting even as they fell back into their mountain strongholds and then into other, still more arid areas of the colony. They became skilled in stocktheft, raiding the colonists' sheep and cattle, sometimes driving off entire herds under cover of darkness. When pursued by the colonists, they resorted to the tactic of slaughtering or maiming the stolen animals, one by one, in order to discourage the pursuers. This not only provoked the colonists to a pitch of fury in their reprisals, but it also gave apparent substance to yet another stereotype, soon to gain widespread currency in the Cape and elsewhere: the conviction that the Bushman was in fact a monster of vindictiveness, gratuitous cruelty, and cunning.

That his motives for stocktheft were principally hunger and only secondarily vindictiveness and retaliation was quickly obscured or ignored. That such vindictiveness was not part of the Bushman's natural disposition—as the historian Stow was to note, it was "rather a developed feeling which gradually took possession of his heart: it was the outcrop of desolation and despair"—went equally disregarded. Each act of retribution by the Bushmen only reinforced the earlier, denigratory images that had been imposed on them. Their tactics now provided the whites with a further justificatory theory for their policy of extermination. So monstrous a foe, cunning in his every dealing, cruel to animals, willing to fight to the death rather than surrender, clearly deserved no better fate than the one he was to receive. Such, at any rate, was the belief which made it all too easy for the colonists to consider themselves perfectly blameless in denying land, freedom, and finally life to the Bushmen.

Although there was a brief period, around the end of the eighteenth century, when several efforts were made to negotiate a peace between the /Xam and the colonists, the former were never sufficiently organized for any general agreement to become binding. In any case, they had long since become aware that any compromise which involved surrendering their land would only ensure the destruction of their way of life and their very identity as a people. Thus they were more or less forced into a stance of obduracy. This is evident in many accounts like that of one particular Bushman leader who was resolved to wage war to the bitter end. Apparently, no inducement could prevail on him or his people to cease from their war of reprisal against the intruding trekboers. His invariable answer was,

> Restore my land, and I will cease from troubling you. Give me back the land of my fathers, and then there shall be peace.

This was not bloody-mindedness. It was the intransigence of the doomed. There would be numerous additional accounts of Bushmen who would fight on to the last arrow and who, even when faced with an inevitable death, would make every effort to cover their heads so that the hated enemy might not see the death agony contort their features. But the many instances of Bushman heroism and self-sacrifice were of no avail. By the early nineteenth century the plight of the /Xam had only worsened, their numbers always less, their world having shrunk by now to that most drought-stricken, inhospitable area of the northern Cape known as Bushmanland. Worse still, this territory began to be invaded by other indigenous groups also in flight from the white colonists, no less intent upon usurping the land left to the /Xam and participating in their slaughter. Around the 1850s, there was an intensification of the already long history of atrocities. In an official report of 1863, Louis Anthing, a recently appointed magistrate in the northern Cape, revealed that "during the last ten years a wholesale system of extermination of the Bushman people had been practiced. Corannas from the Orange River, Kafirs from Schietfontein, colored and European farmers from Namaqualand, Bokkeveld, Hantam, Roggeveld, the districts of Fraserburg and Victoria, and doubtless Hope Town too, all shared in the destruction of these people." Those /Xam that still survived, Anthing emphasized, had become a desperate remnant: "unless something be done to provide them with means of subsistence, they must either steal or perish." His terrible document goes on:

Those Bushmen who went into the service of the newcomers did not find their condition thereby improved. Harsh treatment, insufficient allowance of food, and continued injuries inflicted on their kinsmen are alleged as having driven them back into the bush, from whence hunger again led them to invade the flocks and herds of the intruders, regardless of the consequences, and resigning themselves, as they say, to the thought of being shot in preference to death from starvation.

From their struggle with inhuman power over the previous century and more, only 500 or so /Xam were now left alive. Many of the recent dead had not been shot, as Anthing also noted, but had in fact starved to death. Even so, his report to the colonial government had no material effect. He himself came to be regarded as a trouble-maker and was soon transferred to another part of the country, eventually being forced to resign his position. What he had requested as a matter of dire urgency–that such things as a magistracy be established in Bushmanland, that land be set aside for the /Xam, that food be provided for them–went ignored. In fact, Wilhelm Bleek's informants were to be among the very last generation of /Xam. When his daughter Dorothea traveled through their land in 1910 she found "just a handful of people left here and there." Not long after, there would be no-one left from the group of Bushmen from which //Kabbo, /Han≠kasso and Dia!kwain once came.

III

By now this story of the fate of the /Xam is well known. Dispossessed of the land over which they had moved as hunters and gatherers for centuries, hunted down by the white colonists as if they were wild animals, regarded as little more than vermin by surrounding black tribes, they were virtually extinct, victims of genocide, by the end of the nineteenth century. Today it would be impossible to recover the full reality of their extermination, but there is one unobtrusive fact which suggests the horror and pity of it as well as any other: there is no one left on earth today who can speak the /Xam language. Worse still, no one is in a position to gain a fully reliable knowledge of it, even if he or she wished to.

This one fact not only suggests the extent of the destruction visited upon them–it was, in effect, total–but also some of the problems facing anyone who wishes to translate or re-translate the material that W. H. Bleek and Lucy Lloyd were able to transcribe. There no longer exists a single person to whom one could go in order to clear up a cultural reference, to gain clarity on the possible meanings of a /Xam word, the social function of a myth, and other obscurities. There is not even a comprehensive grammar or dictionary available; *A Bushman Dictionary*, finally published in 1956 by Bleek's daughter, Dorothea, remains incomplete. At best the present-day translator has to rely on clues provided by anthropologists, archeologists and scholars of rock art if he or she is to gain sufficient insight into the material even to make a beginning. While many of these findings are invaluable, any translator from the /Xam has always to set to work in the face of one corrosive certainty: he or she does not know, and knows it can never be known, whether an interpretation–and all translation is interpretation–is entirely faithful to the original, to the letter or the spirit.

In a sense this might not matter. It has been said many times already that all translation condemns one, willy-nilly, to some degree of infidelity towards the original text. Working with /Xam material, however, this age-old dilemma is more sharply posed. Here, it is not a question of whether one betrays or not; given the nature of the material, one is more or less fated to do so, both unconsciously and consciously. And, if there is any excuse at all for one's betrayals, it is to be found only in the type of end one seeks to achieve.

In my case, this has been relatively straightforward. Throughout these translations the chief goal (and indeed justification for my practice) has been dictated by the central problem posed by the material itself: the fact that it is dead, doubly dead. Apart from the isolated attentions of anthropologists and other academic specialists, the astonishing riches contained in the Bleek and Lloyd collection might as well not exist. Accordingly, I have worked to bring the words of the narrators to life once more, and in such a way that they might continue to speak to us who are alive in the last decade of the twentieth century. Although a few of the translations as they appear here are so close as to be almost literal renderings, my goal has inevitably meant that a good number of the poems are 'imitations' (in Robert Lowell's sense of that word) rather than exact word-for-word versions. The /Xam believed that the dead spoke to the living. Without in any way believing that I, as translator, could speak with the tongues of the dead in turn, I have tried to hear the voice of Bleek and Lloyd's three main informants–//Kabbo, Dia!kwain, /Han≠kasso–and create poems which work in the English language. As such, these translations are really extensions of several voices, languages and sensibilities for the sake of a poetry which otherwise might not have existed.

The periphrases, re-writings and re-structurings necessary to achieve my overall goal have, at times, seemed a further betrayal of my originals. Doubly so because the very fact of the /Xam's extinction would seem to demand an absolute measure of fidelity from any translator. But if this knowledge has involved me in many a qualm of conscience, as well as purely technical difficulties, I have also remembered that Kierkegaard's dictum–to the effect that the past which cannot be made present is not worth remembering–applies as much to translation as any other endeavor. For the modern-day reader there would, I believe, be little point in keeping close to that literal English version Bleek and Lloyd give of the first part of the poem translated here as "The Sun, the Moon, and the Knife":

> The moon here is full, the moon lies (in the east) daybreak, she is full/ great the moon, she is living, she lies, the sun sets, he is there the moon lies there for the moon is living the moon becomes (or makes) the great moon the moon mounts the sky yes; for the moon is the great moon.

Without considerable re-writing and re-casting, a piece like this seems fated to remain buried in the past, gathering dust in the archives of the University of Cape Town where its original is on deposit. Similarly, even the modern reader familiar with the kind of syntactical spiralings and deliberate 'word-salads' to be found in a Gertrude Stein would soon find his or her mind blurring under the impact of an extract like the following from the original transcript of "The Girl Who Created the Milky Way':

> She said to the wood ashes: "The wood ashes which are here, they must altogether become the Milky Way. O They must white lie along in the sky, that the stars may stand outside of the Milky Way, while the Milky Way is the Milky Way, while it used to be wood ashes." They (the ashes) altogether become the Milky Way. The Milky Way must go round with the stars; while the Milky Way ( ) feels that, the Milky Way lies going round; while the stars sail along; therefore the Milky Way, lying, goes along with the stars. The Milky Way, when the Milky Way stands upon the earth, the Milky Way turns ( ) across in front while the Milky Way means to wait (?), while the Milky Way feels that the stars are turning back; while the stars feel that the sun is the one who has turned back; he ( ) is upon his path; the stars turn back; while they go to fetch the dawn; that they may lie nicely, while the Milky Way lies nicely.

To make such material accessible I have had to excise, add, re-cast and, not least, re-envision. In the end, there seemed no alternative. One could either remain close to Bleek or Lloyd's literal English version and produce a piece without poetic charge, fated to remain immured in the past; or one could re-work so as to bring the material into the present, living for those alive in the present.

Nevertheless, I have been far from arbitrary in my re-casting of many of the extracts printed here. Although I have on occasion created lines where no such lines existed in the original, though I have at times added circumstantial detail (such as the fact that one of the informants, //Kabbo, was a convict when he once went traveling in a train—an episode recounted in "The Name of My Place"), and although I have necessarily had to impose interpretations on material whose meaning had been left implicit or was only apparent through masses of narrative that had to be excluded—although I have done all this, my practice has not been founded on personal whimsy. I have at all times tried to base my re-writing upon an understanding, derived largely from anthropological writings, of the meaning, as well as the social function, of the particular stories and poems. "the Abandoned Old Woman" has the following conclusion in Bleek's literal prose translation:

> They were obliged to leave her behind, as they were all starving and she was too weak to go with them to seek food at some other place.

My own version becomes:

> It was none of our fault;
> we were all of us starving.
> No one could help it,
> that we had to leave her behind.
> We were all of us starving,
> and she, an old woman,
> she was too weak to go with us,
> to seek food at some other place.

On the face of it, this might seem to be an entirely unwarranted, indeed cavalier, re-writing of the original, dictated solely by poetic purposes and constructed, evidently, in the interests of nothing more than pathos. Yet in the case of "The Abandoned Old Woman," we know from other sources like the work of the anthropologist Roger L. Hewitt, that the /Xam felt understandable guilt and fear about the practice of what he calls "institutionalized geriatricide;" and thus it is not pure guesswork on my part to incorporate in the poem certain elements which might suggest this. Admittedly, this is only one possible interpretation among several, but it is not without foundation. The same can be said, I hope, for all the translations printed in this book.

To translate is to resurrect–linguistically, literally. The Bleek and Lloyd collection is a resource whose many treasures have been unavailable to all but the scholar for far too long. In the hundreds of pages that comprise these archives, much that is left of the poetry of a culture several thousand years old has been preserved. Above all, I have wanted to disinter this poetry, guided by a principle quite simple in all but practice: to make the dead live, to bring back to life. If, on occasion, I have been shameless in my additions to and subtractions from the originals, then I have not been any more so than, say, Ezra Pound in those Chinese poems, entitled *Cathay* (1915), which he translated, with scarcely adequate knowledge of Chinese, from the notes left him by Ernest Fenollosa. These versions have often been attacked by linguists for their many inaccuracies and blatant inventions. But Pound's compatriot, T. S. Eliot, surely understood the former's objectives (as the critics quite often failed to do) when he later spoke, in his introduction to Pound's Selected Poems (1928), of Pound as "the inventor of Chinese poetry for our time." Although the present translator would hardly dare claim a similar role for himself in relation to the /Xam, it is in a similar spirit at least that he has approached his task.

IV

The purely technical problems have been many. One of the most obvious features of the verbal surface of /Xam stories is the frequent repetition (with minor variations) of syntactic and other elements, this being characteristic of oral literatures in many parts of the world. It is a feature which creates an apparent 'circling' rather than linear progression in many of the stories. The translator is under an obligation to preserve at least some of this. At the same time, he or she cannot avoid reducing or thinning it out a little. Written literature often does not tolerate the kind of poetics found in oral forms. What has been called the "repetitive density" of many /Xam narratives can be too rich a diet for modern tastes, producing nothing so much as that effect of blurring which I have already mentioned. Simpler by far was the task of modernizing archaicisms and anachronisms. Not surprisingly, given the time of Bleek and Lloyd's original transcripts, words like "thee" and "thou" abound. In almost all cases I have avoided using them. Unless one has the peculiar ability of an Ezra Pound to combine the ancient and modern in a relationship not antagonistic, these cannot fail to stand out in any poetic texture like stray raisins in a cake not supposed to be made of fruit in the first place.

A more vexing problem was posed by some of the characteristics of poetry in the twentieth century. At the risk of oversimplification, it is fair to say that in the modern world this art has been heavily reliant upon the image (and thus to a large extent on the adjective). In the case of many a /Xam narrative, however, the use of the adjective is very sparing indeed. An effect of bareness, as in a piece like "The Story of Ruyter," is more the rule than the exception. Taking into account twentieth-century conventions (and conventional expectations as to the poetic), as well as this character of the /Xam style of narration, I have had to steer an often ticklish course between the alternatives of excessive adjectival indulgence and abstinence. Nor have I been able to exploit those almost ritualized uses of certain adjectives which one finds, for example, in Homer. In the /Xam world, there would seem to have been relatively few equivalents of phrases like the "wine-dark sea."

A still greater difficulty was presented by the /Xam world-view, in particular the sense of time and logic which the narratives embody. The /Xam language is not like that of the Hopi Indians, for instance, whose verbs make no distinction between past and present, and in which all time runs together in something like an ever-continuing present. Nevertheless, only a brief acquaintance with the material convinced me of the degree to which its sense of time is not our sense, its notion of causation not ours either. Frequently, those words which to us designate cause and effect—words like "therefore"—seem not to indicate anything like the logical relation which we might anticipate. How far to go in reproducing this apparent 'illogic'? Again, given my over-all aims, I found it necessary to be sparing, resisting any excessive, slavish imitation of this feature of the texts. Whatever the losses or gains, it should be remembered that my versions are a good deal 'clearer' and more logically structured than many of their sources.

It may also be noticeable that I have not adopted one single voice or English verse-form for these translations. Although it is often difficult to avoid translating most things into one's own characteristic voice—whether this be a Rilke lullaby or a /Xam prayer to the new moon—both the sheer variety of the material itself as well as the distinction in the styles of the three narrators would seem to justify this. //Kabbo, for instance, rarely gives a complete story from beginning to end; he is much more likely to introduce anything that happens to interest him, wandering from natural history to legend and back again in a kind of "stream of consciousness" (his enthusiasm was particularly aroused by descriptions of practical activities, springbok-hunting most of all.) /Han≠kasso, on the other hand, is notable for the readiness with which he enlivens his narration with songs and chants, while Dia!kwain tends towards the serious rather than the humorous in the manner of his telling. Unfortunately, these very individual characteristics cannot be properly appreciated in the limited number of extracts that appear here; they nevertheless do make the adoption of one voice—and only one tone of voice—a positive limitation.

In addition, it should be mentioned that my versions are often based on excerpts rather than complete narratives. 'The Story of the Dawn's Heart Star," to cite just one instance, runs to several hundred pages; here there was space only for several fragments from it. In this case, as in many others, I have created titles which I deemed to be appropriate. My principle of selection has been both expedient (would this work in English?) and illustrative (does this throw light on one or other aspect of /Xam life?) Needless to say, what has been included does not encompass the full range of /Xam beliefs and customs. With the exception of "The Story of Ruyter," "//Kabbo's Road into Captivity" and a few others, their relations with the white settler population are obviously not fully represented. What I do hope the material and the manner of its arrangement reveals is something of the ever more fateful historical destiny of the /Xam, a movement (as one turns the page) from a time in which the traditional practices and beliefs of the society could still be sustained, down to the contemporary moment in the second half of the nineteenth century when this was becoming less and less possible. This perspective might afford the reader something experienced by the translator in the course of his work: a sense of moving through different types of time, from a mythical dimension to an historical. It might also have the virtue of underscoring the clash between the two as the nineteenth century advanced, the mythical being doomed to disintegrate and then vanish under the onslaught of historical forces.

Most of the transcriptions in the Bleek and Lloyd collection are not cast in verse forms. Why, then, have I sought to re-cast everything, whether a hymn, a myth, or a plain prose account, as poetry? Certainly not in order to suggest that the /Xam were inhabitants of some mythical-poetical Eden. Whilst I have been aware of what could be called, both vaguely and precisely, the 'poetic' nature of some of the original material, it has never been my intention to suggest that these people spoke nothing but poetry. Rather, the mode of poetry seemed particularly suitable as a framing device, above all when dealing with extracts. Moreover, I wanted a form which might lead me, quite consciously, to seek out the poetic–the possible 'poetic idea'–in any single piece and highlight it. Poetry, in short, enabled me to cast into relief certain features which would almost certainly have been lost in even the best prose translation. And, as it happened, the adoption of poetry led not only to a better understanding of certain problems in the translating, but also to a more acute appreciation of some of the stereotypical attitudes which the /Xam and other Bushman groups have had to suffer, whether alive or dead.

V

Several of these stereotypes can still be regarded as temptations, though not all of them are absolute evils. The first of these can be simply put. When one's subject is a people now extinct, exterminated with all the brutality that the word itself implies, it is hard, if not impossible, to avoid the elegiac tone when translating their surviving records. Over and over, the fact of their non-existence insinuates itself into one's consciousness and the mode of elegy itself comes to have the force of gravity whenever one sets to work. All too quickly one sees their own words through the screen interposed by a knowledge of their fate, and its particular terror. As instinctively, perhaps, the temptation arises to exploit all the emotional possibilities in adverbial constructions like "no longer." In one sense this is entirely legitimate; in fact, it is authorized by the usages of several of the narrators themselves. Yet I have had to be wary of that sometimes overwhelming temptation towards elegy and lament that hindsight inspires. No fate has been more terrible than that of the /Xam, even in the fateful context of South African history as a whole. But elegy can also become stereotype. As translator, I found that, repeatedly, I had to prevent my historical knowledge of their fate from insinuating itself even into those pieces which display no awareness of that impending fate.

In the second place there was a far less subtle and infinitely less attractive temptation which arose at various points. This is what I would call "the little Bushman syndrome." Even in a relatively recent and mostly scholarly collection like Philip Tobias's *The Bushmen* (1979), a number of contributors do not seem to be able to refer to the /Xam (or !Kung) without first using the qualifying adjective "little." The /Xam were, of course, of small stature–we know from the prison records that //Kabbo was no more than five feet tall–but a people who enjoyed very little charity while still alive do not deserve the posthumous charity of being sentimentalized as dwarfs. As far as I know, the epithet "little" only occurs in these translations to qualify measurements of time (for example, "a little while" as in the poem "Sun, Moon, and Stars") and not the size of human bodies. And this is as it should be: in not one of these extracts do the informants refer to themselves as "little."

Using the mode of poetry for these translations also cast into relief a more positive temptation. This is what I would call, for want of a better expression, the 'natural surrealism' of so many extracts. This is implicit in several of the titles–"Rain in a Dead Man's Footsteps," "The Meaning of a Sneeze"–as well as in the material itself. The notion that on a person's death a rain will start falling, filling his or her footsteps (as if these were still alive) and so removing all trace of their presence on earth; the belief that one's name can be borne on the wind to places hundreds of miles away; the idea that the corpses of dead people are what fill up the hollow created by the horns of a new moon and thereby make it grow full–such beliefs have a quality which might well lead one to regard those adventures into the bizarre by the historical Surrealists as merely artificial by comparison. This is not to say that the /Xam were Surrealists *avant la lettre*, but that they lived within a structure of beliefs whose horizons did not stand guard over the possibilities of consciousness as they do for us–or at least not in the same way. The temptation to keep the strange strange, the bizarre bizarre, the fantastic fantastic–all the uses of enchantment–has been a constant one throughout this work. More or less instinctively, I have found myself emphasizing just these aspects, often using them as the 'poetic idea' around which the rest of my particular translation might cohere. At the same time I have not forgotten that what might seem chiefly, enchantingly surreal to us–say, the creation of the moon from a veldskoen thrown up into the sky, as in a poem like "The Origin of the Moon"–may well have had a very different meaning for the /Xam themselves.

I could not help being much more wary of another temptation. The conviction has long flourished that there is something like a spirit, an essence, or 'soul of the Bushman', and that this embodies precisely those habits of mind not readily available to us, living in modern technological societies today. I have been wary not because I necessarily disbelieve this; only that I am uncertain as to whether I–despite the convictions that come to translators all the more power-fully given the very nature of their work–have had even partial access to it. Like many others today, I do not live a life interpenetrated by a system of 'magico-religious beliefs and practices,' as the /Xam undoubtedly did. Moreover, I do not speak their language and thus cannot really know the conceptual horizons of their world–for instance, their way of experiencing or feeling time.

Yet there was one thing which I could not avoid. If I have tried to escape some of the more obvious myths about the /Xam, I could not help informing my work through a certain understanding of myth itself. No doubt there are still those who, pointing to the /Xam's relatively primitive technology, would maintain that they lived in a world of illusions, peopled by imaginary spirits and governed by uncomprehended forces, all of them now discredited by scientific and historical criticism. Yet no amount of the latter, I am convinced, really destroys the profound intent of that web of cultural and symbolic meanings which was their mythology. Through their construction of it, the /Xam made the world a home for themselves as surely as through the techniques with which they built their material shelters. It was through myth, above all, that they endowed the world with meaning and, moreover, forged that correspondence between human meaning and a presumed universal order that assuaged their deepest fears, their unanswerable needs. For myth fills the mysterious, often fearful domain of the unknown and the unknowable with more or less likely, but always intelligible, stories. It is, as Thomas Mann once put it, "the garment of mystery." In a world in which nature was hardly benign, human nature never simply given, death an ever-present shadow, there is little doubt that the /Xam's various myths gave them the assurance that their own lives participated directly in some universal, living cosmological order, that the structures of psyche and cosmos were bound tight in a web in which nothing was meaningless, no death final.

Not surprisingly, I found myself having to do something analogous in the actual process of translation or re-translation. Among many other things, this art involves one in an education, often frustrating, in the limits of one's own particular language. To translate is to learn, forcibly, something of the poetic possibilities that one's language enables in any one time and place. These are far from infinite, at least in practice. Perhaps as a result of the artificial circumstances of their narration, many of the narratives in the Bleek and Lloyd collection do not make use of closure in so marked a fashion as other literatures. Some of them peter out or get lost in their own digressions, while others mutate into further stories: "Prayer to the New Moon," which is really a preface to the immediately following account of the origins of death, is a case in point. The /Xam, in short, knew little of the Romantic cliché of the climax. Yet, as translator again, I have been compelled to closure, to find endings for pieces which either did not end or ended in a way which did not seem resonant to my particular ear. In other words, I too have had to 'bind tight' any number of extracts in whatever ways the conventions of the English poetic tradition seemed to allow. In "The Return of the Moon," for example, the final three lines have been taken from a kind of parenthesis which is to be found in the penultimate, not the final, paragraph of the original narrative. In fact, the translating of /Xam material has reminded me that it is often in the manner of concluding a piece, of rounding it off or rounding it out–and the English metaphors are telling–that the greatest betrayals of original meaning might well take place. For it is precisely here that one' s own myths–including the myth of meaning itself–are inclined to take precedence.

Even so, if the art of translation involves the final injustice (some might say second death) of one language's ingestion by another, the attempt itself cannot be forsworn. This is particularly so in the case of the /Xam. In 1929 Dorothea Bleek published an article which makes that act of preservation which is also translation still more imperative, whatever the difficulties and limitations of one's own attempts. Towards the end of it she wrote:

> Fifty years ago every adult Bushman knew all his people's lore. A tale begun by a person from one place could be finished by someone from another place at a later date. In 1910 I visited the northern parts of the Cape Colony and found the children, nephews and nieces of some of the former informants [such as //Kabbo and Dia!kwain] among the few Bushmen still living there. Not one of them knew a single story. On my reading some of the old texts a couple of old men recognized a few customs and said, "I once heard my people tell that." But the folklore was dead, killed by a life of service among strangers and the breaking up of families.

It is finally a knowledge of just this–a tale of unhappiness for which the white people are largely to blame–which has prompted these versions. Through their presentation here, I do not pretend to any political role for myself. No series of poems could even begin to right an historical wrong as total, irredeemable, as that inflicted upon the /Xam. But whether the pages that follow evoke that strangely beautiful imagery of sun, moon, and stars as it appears and reappears in various creation myths, or serve to record the brutality of Ruyter's death at the hands of his white master, it is my hope that in them at least some echo of the /Xam's all-important presence on this earth may still be heard.

Stephen Watson

Song of the Broken String

In a Far-Off Place

In that place, far-off, where //Kabbo once lived,
the sorcerers, dancing, would fall into a trance.
Wanting us to believe they were no longer men,
our sorcerers would turn themselves into birds
and we really believed that they were those birds.

In //Kabbo's place, far-off, and still farther,
it happened if a sorcerer wanted to kill us
he would change himself, evilly, into a jackal.
To us, there, our magicians really were jackals.
We lived there, where a man could really be this.

We lived, then, in a world of men become birds.

[handwritten annotations: "very familiar", "against your will maybe", "Spacial & temporal distance evoked", "ritual", "Can't turn to system of belief", "similar to nostalgia or loss of innocence"]

The Rain-Sorcerer

He was of our family, the man we called //Kunn.
He was a rain's man; he used to make rain.
He made the rain's hair, the kind falling softly.
He made the rain's legs, falling only in columns.
He would summon the cloud, this sorcerer of rain.

//Kunn could make rain come out of the west.
When he lived to the north, a mountain Bushman,
the rain from the west would always turn north.
//Kunn could make rain, he could move rain
to the place where he lived, in the mountains.

He was one of us, this sorcerer of rain.
But he lived to the north, we to the east.
Both his father, his mother, were unknown to me.
//Kunn was old even then, when I was a child.
He was very old then. He is long since dead.

He no longer dances, catching the rain-animal.
His heart no longer falls down, into the water-pit,
fetching the rain-bull, the rain in its wake.
He no longer leads it across the parched flats,
scattering its meat, its blood and milk become rain.

He was the last that I knew, this rain-sorcerer.
He was the very last, the man we called //Kunn–
this maker of rain, and the scent of the rain,
this sorcerer of water, of the fragrance of grass,
sorcerer of rain's hair, summoner of clouds.

Rain in a Dead Man's Footsteps

When a person dies
a rain starts falling,
filling, erasing his living footsteps,
filling the hollows
of a dead man's footsteps
so the footsteps themselves
will no longer be there.

When we have put
him into the ground,
put him down into his grave,
the rain comes to wash
his footsteps' hollows;
all trace is erased
of the spoor that we knew.

Even when
we have not yet covered
the grave with cut bushes,
before we have piled
stones on cut bushes
(so the bushes themselves
will not lie there naked),

A rain starts falling,
filling his footsteps;
there is rain erasing
the footsteps that were his,
rainwater destroys
that by which he was known,
there is rain
in a dead man's footsteps.

Sun, Moon, and Stars

The sun that is down
comes out of the mountains.
It will stand there, above us,
high in the heavens. Come morning,
the sun will once more go
walking across the great skies.

The moon, hunter's moon,
will come out of that mountain;
it too will go walking, waxing
and waning across the great skies.

The star we await,
that star will come after, out of the mountain;
it will climb, quick like the others,
rising, striding, across the great skies.

Many stars are in heaven;
there are whole clans of people –
men, women, and children –
long since become stars.

And now the star woman,
see, she starts rising,
comes again like a mother
leading out her star child,
while the man star follows,
his star child running after.

If the sun is long down,
if the young moon has set,
the star mother will come,
come out of the mountain,
will still lead her star child –
even if, as you see,
he runs away for a while,
runs now, for a little, into a cloud.

Prayer to the New Moon

Moon now risen, returning new,
take my face, this life, with you,
give me back the young face, yours,
the living face, new-made, rising:

O moon, give me the face
with which you, having died, return.

Moon forever lost to me,
and never lost, returning;
be for me as you once were
that I may be as you:

Give me the face, o moon,
which you, having died, make new.

Moon, when new, you tell us
that that which dies returns;
your face returning says to me
that my face, dead, shall live:

O moon, give me the face
which you, your death, makes new!

The Sound of the Stars

When I slept at my grandfather's, in his hut,
I would sit with him, outside in the cool.
I would ask him about the sound which I heard,
which I sometimes seemed to hear speaking.
He'd say it was stars that were speaking.
"The stars say Tsau! They say Tsau! Tsau!"
They are cursing the springbok's eyes, he'd say.
"This is the sound that stars like to make;
and summer's the time they like to sound."

When at my grandfather's, I listened to stars.
I could hear the sound, the speech of the stars.
Tsatsi would say it was these that I heard,
that they were cursing the springboks' eyes
to help us in hunting, in tracking down game.
Later, when full-grown, and a hunter as well,
I was the one who listened, still listened.
I could sit there and hear it come very close:
the star-sound Tsau, sounding Tsau! Tsau!

Throwing Fire at the Stars

Canopus appearing, our people call to a child:
"Bring us some wood, the stick over there;
let us set it alight at the edge of the fire,
let us point it, aflame, towards Sirius, the star."
We /Xam say to the man who first sees her rise:
"You must take a stick, point it burning at her,
that the sun may come out and may shine for us,
so Sirius, this star, will not come out coldly,
so she will bear Bushmen's rice, a promise of food."

And whoever first sees her then goes to his son:
"Bring me that stick, the one you see there,
let me fire its one end, burn it towards Sirius,
let me aim it like this, burning at Sirius,
all the while praying that she rise like Canopus."
And he takes the lit brand brought by his son.
He points it, alight, flames blowing towards Sirius,
mouthing his prayer, that it shine as the other.

He sings. He sings of Canopus, sings about Sirius,
pointing the fire till each shines like the other.
He brandishes the stick; he throws fire at the stars.
Till exhausted by this, his stick burnt to ashes,
he lies down, exhausted, kaross covering his head.
He has worked to bring Sirius into the sun's warmth,
worked this hard that a star will come out, not coldly,
so the women can go out early, looking for Bushmen's rice,
as they walk out now, the sun on their shoulder-blades.

The Girl Who Created the Milky Way

The stars turn back, white, when they turn towards dawn.
The stars always turn back while they go to fetch dawn.
They stand there in the sky, pale, above the horizon;
they pause for a while, they wait there, white-faced,
before they continue, follow the star footprints,
the paths which all stars must sail to their setting.

My mother said a girl had made them like this,
that the girl of the Early Race, in her house of illness,
angry with her own mother, hungry for more !huin roots,
had got up one day, scooped her hands full of ashes.
She threw them into the sky, she commanded them then:
"You ashes of wood, which I have held in my hands,
you will be what I say, will become the Milky Way.
You will lie there, a white arc, encircling the heavens,
white like wood ash, the other stars standing separate.
The wood ashes you were will now be you, Milky Way,
going round with the stars, with the stars that stand round you,
who must run with the others, turn back, and sail on!"

So the stars must turn back when they go to fetch dawn.
The Milky Way, lying there, must always come back
to the place where the girl first threw up the ashes.
In that long time before us, after she made them,
the sky lay there, still; but the stars moved against it,
sailed on to their setting, following the sun's path.
In silence they floated against a sky standing silent,
always following their courses, turning back in the dawn,
turning white in each dawn when the sun first rises.

After the girl, the first girl of the Early Race,
scooped handfuls of wood ash, threw them into the sky,
the Milky Way must turn back, pale against sunrise,
the Milky Way must climb, a white arc, crossing the heavens.
When the darkness comes out, and other stars glow red,
it stands white in its arc, its own starlight white,
clearing a path for all stars to sail on in the dark.

After the girl in her anger, that girl in her hunger
made the Milky Way out of some handfuls of ashes,
we, the people on earth, can go out in night's darkness,
the earth glowing before us, not covered in darkness.
The people like us, returning home in soft starlight,
guided by starlight, the far white glowing overhead,
we know that she made it to bring us a small night-light,
made the Milky Way glow white, whiter than wood ash,
that we who come after could go home in the dark.

The Sun, the Moon, and the Knife

The moon is still full, still alive
as she hangs in the sky just before dawn.

As soon as the sun goes down in the west,
the moon in the east grows ever fuller,
she climbs the sky, her face more burnished,
her belly swelling, full of moon-children,
travelling the sky from one end to the other,
climbing the night from the eastern quarter
till she hangs here, huge, still full, still alive,
shining in the west just as day breaks.

And as soon as the sun comes up in the east,
he reaches far over the length of the earth.
He swiftly pierces the moon's flesh with his knife
till she who is full, and shining, and alive,
this moon who has speech now has to cry out:
"Sun, leave my children, leave them alone!
Your knife is murdering my unborn moon-children.
The blade of your light stabs our light to death.
Let them still live! Let me, the moon, shine!"

She calls this out while still full in the sky,
still alive in the dawn, before she starts fading.
You can hear her call quickly, hear her cry out
when, each day beginning, the sun lifts up,
takes up his knife to kill her moon-children.
She calls out with a cry, a cry so piercing
that it almost breaks the blade of first light.
Each day she cries out, "Sun, leave my children!
Don't make them die!" And day has broken.

What Happens When You Die

The wind when we die, our own wind blows.
For we, the /Xam people, each of us owns a wind;
each one has a cloud that comes out when we die.
Therefore the wind when we die, the wind blows dust
covering the tracks, the footprints we made
when walking about living, with nothing the matter,
when we still knew nothing of sickness and death.

If not for this wind, our spoor would still show,
our spoor would still show us, as if we still lived.
Therefore our wind has one purpose, erasing our tracks.
Therefore, when we die, our gall sits high above,
our gall sits, when we're dead, green in the sky.

Therefore our mother liked to teach, liked to say
when the moon goes to lie down, stands hollow:
"The moon which you see carries people just died.
You can see for yourselves how it goes to lie down,
can see it lies emptied, horns curved, hollowed out—
it is killing itself because carrying the dead.

"This is why, when hollow, the moon brings bad omens.
You can always expect to hear something, an omen,
when the moon, as you see it, goes to lie down.
You can expect to hear that someone has died,
that a person has just died and the moon grows hollow
to carry him now in the catching-place of its horns."

The Nature of /Kaggen

/Kaggen, old trickster, magician, also called Mantis,
maker of the moon, of the eland, and also of trouble,
though you lie in the fire, your flesh now on fire,
though you lie there writhing in the coals' red heat,
your skin blistered, in tatters, your bones blackening fast
(and how you deserved it, you scoundrel, always picking a fight!)–

You can still change the world by dreaming the world,
you still have your tricks, old unteachable, untamable;
you could still make an eland from a piece of old shoe,
you could still create the moon from an old, bent shoe;
old incorrigible, magician, old /Kaggen you slyboots,
your Hartebeest children, the quivers for your arrows
could still fly to you, unaided, at no more than a word!–

Even then old trickster, young trickster, even there in that fire,
your arms sprouted feathers, you flew out of the flames;
even then, in that heat, you conjured feathers amidst fire,
you flew out of its blistering to wet your burnt flesh;
O survivor of fire, of hot coals, old rascal even then
you again found the water-pool to wash off your feathers,
you flew free, unlike us, once more cock of the walk,
you flew free, your limbs feathered, a bird's, unlike ours,
you flew off, unlike us, your arms working like wings!

The Dawn's Heart Star: Two Fragments

I

We, who are stars, we must walk the sky;
we two, Dawn's Heart Star, Dawn's Heart Child
being part of the heavens, we belong to the sky.

We are heaven's things. Mother is the earth's.
She walks the earth, she sleeps on the ground.
She must walk on the earth, must walk in the night,
a thing of the earth, a beast of prey, eating flesh,
lighting the black earth with eyes that are yellow,
wife of Dawn's Heart, the Lynx, thing of darkness.

Old father moon is cold, is also dark's thing.
He himself walks in darkness, cold in the coldness.
A hide shoe is cold, and he is a hide shoe.
He is darkness's hide shoe thrown into the sky,
a bent veld-shoe, frosty, making light in the dark–
the hide shoe of the Mantis, the moon is cold.

II

"I am the day star, my name is Dawn's Heart.
I shine brightest towards dawn, I stand red
in the red sky that spreads before daybreak.
Thus I too am red, am like a fire that is red.
And you, you are like a small fire, a fire's child:
you are the Dawn's Heart Child, my small star.
And I, your father, who has made a child of his heart,
so I bury you, swallow you, small heart, as a star."

And thus the /Xam say: "we are the Dawn's Hearts."
/Xam of the plains say: "we are of the Dawn's Heart.
We climb to the sky to become the sky's things.
We look to the sky that we may walk there, rise up.
In truth we go round there, above in the sky.
In truth we remain there, walking round in the sky.
We live there, afloat; we do not live on the earth."

Song of the Dawn's Heart Star

Because we are stars
we must walk the sky,
we, both of us stars,
things of the heavens.

But Mother, the Lynx,
is a thing of the earth,
she must walk on the earth,
go to sleep on bare ground.

But we, who are stars,
we cannot go sleeping,
we must walk the sky
unsleeping, awake.

Because we are stars,
because we walk the sky,
we must go round forever,
sleepless, unsleeping.

Things of the heavens.
Stars. Heaven's things.

Blue Mist Like Smoke

The hare
is like a mist,
like !kho,
a blue mist
resembling smoke,
our mothers used to say.

When a mirage
appears at daybreak,
just before sunrise,
they say it is
the hare,
the mirage in it,
that keeps the sun in mist,
that cloaks the sun in smoke,
that weakens the sun's eye,
that does not let it rise,
and brings much illness to us.

It is, they say,
the hare that does it,
a hare like mist,
a hare like smoke,
the mirage in it,
the !kho of it.

It is, they say,
a smoke resembling mist,
blue mist like smoke
that does it.

The Origin of the Moon

The moon was a shoe, veldskoen of the Mantis,
long ago in a time when the Mantis still wept.
The creature he'd made, the Eland he loved,
had been killed by the Meercat, cut into pieces,
and he, poor Mantis, had fought back in a rage.
He was punished for this, forced to fetch wood,
piling wood, and more wood, on the Meercat's fire.

The moon, once a shoe, was not yet in the sky
when the Mantis, still heartsore, happened to see
the gall of the Eland lying unnoticed. Knowing
he could escape if he pierced it clean through,
if the gall was broken and darkness poured out,
he pierced till it burst, leapt into its dark,
but lost his way, blinded, in a tangle of bush.

So he took off his shoe, threw it into the sky.
He said: "I am the Mantis, I am called Mantis,
but my shoe up there, shining red in the dark,
will now be the moon, will shine as the moon,
lighting a path through the dark of the bushes,
lighting the earth, that I may return home."

The sun is white—white because it is hot.
And the stars are very red because they are cold.
But the moon is a shoe, veldskoen of the Mantis.
It is covered in red dust, being a Mantis veld shoe.
It has the dust on it of his walking on earth.
And this is why the moon, once a shoe, glows red.

A Feather Thrown into the Sky

Now groping along, gall caking his eyes,
groping in darkness, the Mantis at last found
this thing in his mouth, sucked into his mouth,
this feather with which he cleaned his caked eyes—
the one which, with these words, he cast high:

"You will remain there, always, above the horizon.
You will now be the moon, your duty to shine,
to shine for us all, lifting night's darkness.
You are the one who must light up each night,
who must lessen the dark under which people live.

"The sun is the one who surrounds us with light.
It brings heat in the day, the daylight day-long.
It is above, this light, under which people walk.
It is above us, this light, in which people hunt.
It is above us, the sun, under which we go home.

"But you are the moon; you give us your light
when falling, falling off, you return alive.
This is what you must do, always falling away,
returning, again living, to shine for us men.
You are the moon. And this the moon's task."

Song of Four Winds

I

Wind come whistling out of the north,
bearing the cloud, grown huge, before it,
blowing the clouds as if from beneath them—
you are the wind that leaves them laden,
that sends them, afloat, far into the south,
you, the north wind, blowing from beneath,
who blow the clouds as if from below them.

II

O wind which lies in the west,
you the one who blows the rain's cloud,
who blowing turns back the rain's cloud
till they lie far, out of reach in the east
you are the one who lies in the west,
you are the west wind of this world.

III

It is the one blows, the south wind,
always a headwind, standing ahead,
the one full in the face, stirring up dirt—
the south wind, uttering nothing but dust.

IV

And you, wind which lies in the east,
O you are hardly a little, weak wind,
blowing cold, your dust dry and cold,
you who have your house in the east,
who send us hurrying to make shelters,
to build windbreaks, to light fires,
our faces to the flames, our hands
held against you, east wind blowing
cold and still colder—dry and cold!

What is the Moon?

The sun is one thing, being warm.
The moon is another, being cold.
The moon is quite different.

The stars also are other.

They are so many, they are red.
And yet they too are cold
with all their star children—
these stars made so many
by their many star children;
all red, all cold
and made cold, these stars,
by running there, in the sky,
all over the depths of the sky.

The sun is warm, the one who is white.
The moon is quite different, cold.

The sun is hot but the moon is cold.
And she is cold, our moon, because she is red.

The Maiden and the Rain

At first it seemed no more than some mist.
She saw it only as one strand of mist
brought by the wind, carried into the sky.
And she went on digging, her home nearby,
went on searching for a little more food,
at first not aware a storm was so close.

"Yet how is it," she thought, looking again,
"that the mist is now cloud, covering the sky?
How is it that that small, thin strand of mist
has suddenly grown huge, a dark beast of prey?
I must leave off digging, go tell my brother
there's a whirlwind's sound, a storm close by!"

But her mother was waiting, ready to scold.
"Have I not told you—and how many times—
you should never go out when kept to your hut?
Your scent still has that strong buchu smell
we give to new maidens to keep them from !Khwa.
You must never go out without being cleansed!"

But it came all the same: rain crashed down.
Wind came in a rush, capturing the maiden,
carrying her with it, sucked up in its blast.
Wind took the maiden higher and higher,
rain's lightning struck just where she stood—
where she, once a girl, was changed to a snake.

Again rain's lightning slashed at the earth;
a whirlwind of dust spiraled into the sky.
The maiden rose with it, earth flying around her,
her mother calling to those that were spared:
"Look, the dust lifts, smoking beneath rain!
Where is my child? Lost, lost in that wind!"

And the sorcerers sing, they still like to say:
"See how a maiden, disobeying her mother,
can be taken by rain, whirled into the sky;
how the rain in its anger takes one forever;
will still take all those who do as she did,
and make of a maiden a thing like a snake!"

Rainmaking with a Bow-String

While we were sleeping, /Kaunu would sit.
He struck his bow-string, cloud coming out.
He plucked out a rhythm that summoned the cloud,
and we woke in the cloud, the sun shut out.

We would hear a far twanging, coming from cloud.
We would wake to find we were sleeping in cloud.
And a rain would begin, lasting into the sunset;
the rain would pour down through two sunsets.

While we were sleeping, /Kaunu sat there, awake.
He made the rain fall by striking his bow-string.
And we woke in the clouds, a sound in the clouds,
cloud pouring out of the sound of a bow-string.

The Abandoned Old Woman

Our mother, old, unable to walk,
lay there, incapable,
alone in her old grass and reed hut.

Before we, her sons,
were obliged to leave her behind,
we blocked up her hut's sides,
closing the openings used as a door,
making use of the struts
from the other huts we were leaving,
but leaving the roof open, exposed to the sky,
so she could still feel
some warmth from the sun.

We had made a small fire.
We had gathered for her
as much dry wood as we could.

It was none of our fault;
we were all of us starving.
No-one could help it,
that we had to leave her behind.
We were all of us starving,
and she, an old woman,
she was too weak to go with us,
to seek food at some other place.

The Anger of the Moon

My father was the one
who told us, always,
that when the sun sets
and the sky glows red,
at just about the time
the moon begins to climb,
I must remember, always,
to keep my eyes downcast;
I must never, ever,
let moonlight touch my eyes
when the moon first rises
from behind the mountain.

For this, he told,
would always make it angry.
And in its moon's anger,
enraged by us who stared,
it would cast us into darkness,
throw us far into the cold
of the cold shadows moonlight
casts behind the bushes
when it first rises, red,
into the darkening sky.

And we were always
much afraid in darkness,
is what he'd say to me.
For darkness resembles fear,
is what he'd always say.
When trees and bushes
are cast into that dark,
we people would grow scared
of the darkness in them,
by this anger of the moon
that places darkness in them.

And this is why
he'd tell me, teach me
that what I must always do,
must promise him to do,
when the moon first rises
behind the darkened mountain,
is lie down against the earth,
my face pressed into my hands,
hands pressed into the earth,
and never lift my eyes
until the moon is there
in the very middle of the night,
the earth below it lightened,
all the bushes softly lit.

For the lion's spoor
was always there, he'd say.
And the moon was always there
ready, if ever looked at,
once above the mountain rim,
to cast us far into that dark
resembling fear, our fear.
And then there'd be no peace.
For us who lay there, in the dark,
there'd be no peace, he'd say.
And there was never any peace.
There was no peace for us,
my father always said.

Catching a Porcupine

Father used to say
if I were out hunting,
having to sit waiting,
waiting for a porcupine,
the time is always best
when the Milky Way turns back–
this is the time
when a porcupine returns.

Father also said
I should feel the wind.
He used to say
I should be careful
always to taste
the direction of the wind.
The porcupine is not a thing
which will return, he'd say,
coming with the wind.
Rather, it moves
slant-wise, across it,
so that it can better
sniff the air and tell
if danger lurks ahead.

Father used to say
I should breathe softly
when sitting, waiting
for a porcupine.
It is a thing, he said
which hears everything.
I must not even
make a rustling.
I must sit deadstill.

Father taught me
about the stars.
He used to say
that whenever I
was sitting by a burrow,
I should watch the stars,
the places where they fell.
I should, above all,
watch them keenly,
for the places where stars fall,
he often taught,
really are the places
where porcupines can be caught.

The Rain that Is Male

The rain that is male is an angry rain.
It brings with it lightning loud like our fear.
It brings water storming, making smoke out of dust.

And we, we beat our navels with our rigid fists.
We, we press a hand, flat to the navel.
We snap our fingers at the angry, male rain.

And we stand outside in the force of the water,
we stand out in the open, close to its thunder,
we snap our fingers and chant while it falls:

"Rain, be gone quickly! Fall but be gone!
Rain, turn away! Turn back from this place!
Rain, take your anger, be gone from our place!"

For we want the other, the rain that is female,
the one that falls softly, soaking into the ground,
the one we can welcome, feeding the plains—

So bushes sprout green, springbok come galloping.

Presentiments

A presentiment
is that thing which we fear
when something is happening,
near or far, at some other place.

A presentiment is like
a dream which we dream.

Sometimes
when we are alone,
our body starts up, shaken–
it seems as if, to the body,
something was there
which the body feared.

And we pass it,
we who are /Xam,
because our body is telling us:
there is danger at that place.

Sneezing Out a Lion

When you hear the call, the "hn-hn-hn" of the owl,
it may be a sorcerer, not the sound of an owl.
He may be snoring a person, getting rid of the owl.

A sorcerer, like this, can also sound like a lion.
When snoring a person, he can roar "han-a, han-a!"
The lion roars "han-a!," and he echoes "hm-m, hm-m."

And the people hear him and follow that sound.
They are waiting to give him their buchu to sniff,
to watch him inhale it, and sneeze out a lion.

A sorcerer may bite us, enraged in his trance.
He may run into the dark, have to be calmed.
But he knows that a lion can enter the flesh,

He knows, having roared, that the lion is no more,
that the lion in the flesh is gone from the flesh,
that having sniffed buchu, the lion is sneezed out.

He knows his patient can be healed by a sneeze,
that a sick man can get up, go hunting again—
as he would once, when the springbok were passing.

Sorcerers Are Like Lions

If a person, good-looking, suddenly falls ill,
and seeming to improve, suddenly grows sicker,
sorcerers have seized him: he dies, seized.

Sorcerers are like lions, their eyes like lions.

And when the dogs at night, restless, keep barking,
sorcerers are coming to work their bewitchment:
it means they're coming close to shoot a sick man.

Sorcerers are like lions, their eyes like lions.

Though the thing is unseen which strikes the sick man,
though invisible arrows are the ones they fire,
these arrows are fatal: they can lay a man dead.

Sorcerers are like lions, their eyes like lions.

Although others try healing, removing harm's things,
a sorcerer still shoots him under their noses.
And thus his heart falls: his heart falls down.

Sorcerers are like lions, their eyes like lions.

The Powers of the Dead

All people
become spirit people
when they die.
My grandfather
used to call them thus,
he used to call them
"the spirit people."

He used to say,
"You have spoken
out loud
the old people's names,
as if these were not
spirit people, dead people.
And so they visit us.
Because of this
they visit us to harm us.
Because people like this,
all spirit people,
they no longer possess
their thinking-strings—
they have
no understanding."

And this is why
they like to come
through the dark to harm us
if we so much as utter
their names by night.
And we dream about them,
we have bad dreams,
nightmares,
if we utter
their names in the dark.

And this is why
we children
dare not utter
the names by night.
Only when the sun is high,
in full daylight,
only then do we children
dare speak their names.

We know
what my grandfather knew:
that all people
become spirit people
when dead,
that their powers live on
long after their death.

The Wind Is One with the Man

Even in summer, when the Pleiades come out,
when the eye of the sun is burning, whitening,
and the plains of our place are dry, dry as horn;
even then, when these stars, the Pleiades, come out,
and being summer stars, what we call summer's things,
they burn small, very white, in our night skies—
the wind, even then, the wind is one with the man.

"The wind," we say then, "is one with the man
who is cold, grown cold, with what he has killed."
"For the one who has killed," we say, "grows cold
with the cold, the wind, of that which he has killed."
Thus we say, even then, in summer we can say:
"Our brother there, his wind blows, blows cold.
It feels like this, cold, because he has killed.
Because the wind, a man's wind, is one with the man."

It is one with him should he look at a star.
The wind that blows from a star, come summer,
will soon blow colder, though it be summer.
That star grows cold, its wind blowing cold.
Because he who looked at it—the man is cold.
Because the wind of he who has killed is cold.
Because the wind, his wind, is one with the man.

Thus we say—it is our /Xam custom to say—
should a man kill a thing, his wind grows colder.
It will blow up dust, much dust, should he kill.
Then the star grows cold, should he look at it;
the wind from the star blows more and more cold.
Though it be the Pleiades, these, summer's things;
the star-wind will start blowing colder against us—
because the wind, this wind, is one with the man.

Jackal Clouds

When a smell of new rain comes with the wind,
when the rain's scent comes blowing along with the wind,
then the jackals appear, lying there to the south.

When, far in the south, the clouds start darkening,
their bellies growing black, black with new rain,
we say "jackal" to the clouds that are building there.

And we watch as they come, a cool wind following.
We watch the jackal shadows crossing the plains,
then the rain that starts letting its apron fall.

We see the springbok running before the wind.
We say: "Clouds are crossing our hunting-grounds,
bearing their danger, their blackness foul-smelling."

For these jackal clouds come to shut out the sun.
Out on the hunting-grounds we fear these dark clouds,
black, blacker than jackals, darkening the sun.

But when, in our hut, with its roof newly laid,
when children have packed the roof with fresh "asbos,"
with walls bound tight so no wind blows through–

Then we wait for the rain, for the apron of rain,
safe from the cloud we call jackals. We sit ready
for it now, for the first downpour. And we love it.

The Lost Tobacco Pouch: A Song

Because I, //Kabbo, have lost my tobacco pouch,
because a dog has run off with it in the night,
and awake in the dark, wandering round in the dark,
I can find it nowhere, yes nowhere, I sing:

> *Famine it is,*
> *tobacco-hunger it is,*
> *famine is here!*

Because there was nothing to do but lie down,
because I could do nothing, not even sleep,
and getting up early, even wandering around early,
I could still find it nowhere, I sing, and must sing:

> *Famine it is,*
> *tobacco-hunger it is,*
> *famine is here!*

Our Blood Makes Smoke

We would know it by our blood, my father used to say,
our blood starting to mist, our blood making this smoke,
that out there in the mists, very early in the morning,
our camp still lost in sleep, a white commando loomed.

We would know it by our bodies, by a blood within
which trembling, shaking, would start to make the smoke,
a smoke which then would sit before us, burning in our eyes—
it was by blood, by smoking blood, we knew the danger near.

Thus we heard the horses, long before we heard their hooves.
Thus we smelt the gunfire, long before the bullets flew.
A commando was upon us, so our blood's smoke foretold.
We would know it by our blood: that day there would be war.

And we fought back fiercely, through our smoking blood.
We would fight back in the mist, armored by this blood.
We fought on until we knew, till our blood also knew,
its smoke clearing at last, the white men were beaten back.

And we were left there then, with our exhausted blood.
Afterwards we were left there, finding our own bodies,
our blood used up, exhausted, in foretelling all we'd see:
earth wet with the wounded, our dead lying all around.

But it was by blood Xaa-ttin, my father, used to say,
in blood, our bodies' smoking, we knew what came for us.
Our blood made mist, our blood made smoke, he'd say,
the day of a white commando, each day our end drew near.

The Story of Ruyter

Ruyter, brought up by white men—Ruyter died
amidst white men at a place called Springkaan's Kolk.
He was bound to a wagon with straps from the oxen;
they tied him face-down because of herding the sheep.
Then the Boer who was master, the Boer began beating
him with the riem that they use for tying a beast.
He said Ruyter, the herder, had not herded well.
This happened, this beating that led to his death.
The Boer hit him and hit him; the other Boers too.
When at last they unloosed him, Ruyter, he fainted.
Those who were there—they all must have known,
they must have known then, when picking him up,
that Ruyter, the herder, was near beaten to death.

This happened. He, Ruyter, said to those people,
he said white people did not believe he felt pain;
they would not believe he felt half-beaten to death.
But to him, to himself, it did not seem he could live.
He kept whispering, repeating, "I looked after the sheep.
I, Ruyter, looked after the sheep." He kept saying
the pain was such, so bad, he could not last long.

It was he, Ruyter, who told the white people there
that his body's middle, here, ached badly, very bad.
It was he who tried still to walk without help.
But the Boer, his master, the one whom he served,
had trampled his body while beating his body.
And Ruyter, before dying, the white men around him,
Ruyter said: "the Boer has broken my body's middle."

40

Song of the Broken String

Because
of a people,
because of others,
other people
who came
breaking
the string for me,
the earth
is not earth,
this place is
a place now
changed for me.

Because
the string is that which
has broken for me,
this earth
is no longer
the earth to me,
this place
seems no longer
a place to me.

Because
the string is broken,
the country feels
as if it lay
empty before me,
our country seems
as if it lay
both empty before me,
and dead before me.

Because
of this string,
because of a people
breaking the string,
this earth, my place
is the place
of something—
a thing broken—
that does not
stop sounding,
breaking within me.

repetition

enjambment

string represents voice? spirit?

idea of string unraveling

Xaa-ttin's Lament

My father sang: the string is broken;
things have changed from what they were.
He sang: "I cannot hear the ringing now
I once used to hear, sounding in the sky."
He sang: "I feel the string has gone from me;
the song is gone: for me things do not change.
Sleeping, no sound comes calling in my sleep.
I cannot hear a voice, the voice once with me,
which would come calling through my dreams."

It said: "Xaa-ttin, are you so sunk in sleep
that you can't call, don't speak to me
as you once would, and loved to do,
when you were with me as my pupil?
Xaa-ttin, I have waited for your word,
a single word that said you were not dead.
O Xaa-ttin, I have listened long for you,
to learn you still lead out the rain-bull.
Tell me you make rain, as I once taught you to!"

My father sang, the string has broken,
that nothing was as he'd once heard it.
He sang: "I cannot hear the ringing now
I once heard often, the sorcerer still alive."
He sang: "I fear the string has gone from me,
that things are changed, and cannot call me.
Sleeping, I cannot hear—I cannot hear it.
There is silence where a song would ring.
There is nothing now, where it once sounded."

//Kabbo's Road into Captivity

I

I came from there. I came from that place,
captured while eating a springbok with my band.
I came here to the Cape, from my place Bitterpits,
captured by the black policemen who bound us to a wagon.

I was there. My wife, my son, were also there.
My son's wife was there, carrying a small child.
My daughter was also there, a small child on her back.
My daughter's husband too. The black men came
and captured us at a time our band was small.

And thus we came, three men bound in a wagon,
our wives following on foot. We came like this
through one day, through the heat of the first day,
till the wagon halted, and we were at last let down.
Thus passed the first of many nights: we made a fire,
roasted the springbok killed earlier with my arrow;
then lay awake, smoking, waiting for daybreak.

There were three of us—three men bound together—
lying in a wagon, being taken to the magistrate.
While the wagon ran, through the next day's heat,
our wives ran on beside it, quickly losing ground.
The wagon ran that day, running faster, faster,
leaving the women running after, unable to keep up.

II

I was brought to talk to the white magistrate.
Therefore he questioned us till it grew late.
Therefore it was night, and dark, when his men
took us back to jail, and put our legs in stocks.
And thus we lay there, legs locked in the stocks,
hurting from the wood a white man put around them.
We lay there with the others, many Korana convicts.
Thus all of us lay bound, not turning in our sleep,
our legs hurting us until the next day came,

when they gave us flesh, flesh from a boiled sheep.
We ate meat; were bound; travelled on southwards.

We came here then, to work upon the roads.
We were brought to this place, Victoria West.
There we were lifting stones, up to our chests,
were rolling them away. We had to carry earth,
loaded in a hand-barrow, and throw it out again.
We had to do this many days, we and the Koranas.
We had to throw it in a wagon, push the wagon wheels.
There for many days we loaded earth, unloaded earth,
we and the Koranas. And when they took us back
to jail each night, sheep's flesh is what we ate.

III

I came from that place. I came here like this,
on foot to Beaufort West, when the sun was burning,
walking on foot, arms bound to the wagon chain.
We walked, bound, from Victoria to Beaufort jail,
where we got tobacco, smoking it in sheep's bones.
Then we ate more sheep; sheep is what we ate.
And when we slept that night, in a prison there
without a roof, rain fell upon us in the dark.

We came here then, passing through a river,
water splashing on our bodies as we waded it.
We came here upon a road, in the next day's heat,
walking bound to a chain, in the wagon tracks.
We walked until night fell, when a white man came
to lock us in the train we call a "fire wagon."
We boarded in the dark, from that place there,
and did not sleep while all night the train ran on
to this place, to the Cape, its Cape prison-house.

I came here like this. Therefore we came here,
the Koranas and we /Xam, tied to one another.
Therefore I came, a convict, to the Breakwater here.

We came to work on it, leaving our wives behind.
We came to this place here, leaving our place far behind.
We came to work; therefore they gave us sheep's flesh.
But we were tired by then, we were so tired already
we lay down then and there—we lay down to sleep at noon.

The Name of My Place

You have not heard,
I have not told how I,
a convict at that time,
first went travelling in a train,
how I would have fallen out
had not a woman dragged me back,
and how nice it was to sit in it,
the two of us then seated there:
I and one black man.

You have not heard,
nor have I yet said
how his face was black,
how this black man's mouth
was also black;
how the white men are those
whose faces are red,
they being to me
the handsome men.

You have not heard
and I have not yet said
how it was this black man
who asked me then:
"What is your place, its name?"
How I replied, "I come
from that place, called home."
How he asked again,
"Tell me, what is its name?"
And how I, called //Kabbo, said:

"My place is Bitterpits."

What Is Your Name?

Your name, your real /Xam name,
what is it? Call it for me,
say it out loud for me
that I may hear once more
its sound–what it is like.

Tell me, what is your name,
your true /Xam name?
Call it, say it for me.
I long to hear it now,
the sound that it will make.

And do not tell me stories.
Do not now deceive me.
Talk only our own /Xam
that I can truly hear you,
how you speak our only tongue.

But you, a /Xam like us,
you do not tell us plainly.
The country that is yours–
what is its name? I say again:
tell me where you come from.

Your people are at what place?
Tell me where your people live?
Pronounce the place's name for me.
And tell me now, what is your name,
your only name, your true /Xam name!

The Meaning of a Sneeze

I think that /Han≠kasso has seen !Kwaba-an.
I think that he has seen Swaba-//ken.
I think !Kwaba-an calls my name.
I think that Swaba-//ken calls my name.
I think //Goa-ka-!kwi calls my name.

He asks Kerru about me. He asks Kerru,
"Where is //Kabbo?" And Kerru answers,
"Your father, //Kabbo, is with his master."
His mother asks him, and her son says,
"Your husband remains there, with his master.
I think he cannot yet come home to us."

I think that my wife, !Kwaba-an,
has called my name: because I sneeze.
I think that my son, //Goa-ka-!kwi
has called my name: because I sneeze.
I think my daughter, Swaba-//ken,
calls my name: it is because I sneeze.

I think her husband says to her,
I think my daughter's husband says,
"These are your father's trousers;
his master told him to give them to me."
And I think !Kwaba-an, my wife, asks,
"Are these not my husband's trousers?"
He answers, "They were once your husband's."
I think all this because I sneeze.

Seeing them now, I think she says,
I think she says then to our daughter,
"My husband seems to want me with him.
He is surely trying to hear from me.
He is lonely, alone there with his master.
He has lived too long there without his son.
We must go to him, however far from home."
I think all this because I sneeze.

Cows and Twigs

In work-time, daytime, I go to the cow-house.
In work's time, mornings, I take up the rake.
I must clean the pathways, rake up the twigs,
the many small twigs blown down in the night,
that I may not trip up, fall over those twigs,
that small sticks of wood may not capture my feet,
and I may walk without falling when it grows dark,
when I come to eat after dark in my master's house.

In work's time, mornings, I make the paths nicely smooth.
For I must take care when the place is in darkness.
For my work is the cow, fetching water after dark,
carrying the full pail so she may drink in the dark.
I must take care of the twigs on my way to the cow.
For my fear is I may fall, fall over those twigs.
And the cow in the cow-house, what will happen to her?–
The cow in the cow-house, tethered, with no water,

May not grow full, in the dark, of the darkness's milk.

//Kabbo Tells Me His Dream

I dreamed of a lion which talked,
of lions which talked to their fellow-lions.
I heard them, I saw them: in my dream they were black.
Their paws were just like the paws of real lions.
They were covered in hair, their tails were long.
They had so many legs that I saw them, afraid.

I was afraid of them, was frightened awake.
I lay here, like one woken, staring around me.
They were still there, their tails tipped with black,
with so much hair they were shod with black hair.
I heard the lions say they must follow the springbok,
that they must follow the spoor that led faraway,
that led to the place, the plains of my home.

I lay there, woken: I could still see the spoor.
In my dream I saw clearly the springbok once more.
Back in my dream I had seen just how many;
and I saw myself hunting, as I did in the past.
I saw the many tracks, the paths made by their spoor.
I saw the footpaths of spoor–and lay there, staring.

Back in the dream, I dreamed of my wife.
She, !Kwaba-an, had moved somewhere else.
The people were different, the huts had changed.
In the dream she asked me for something to smoke.
But my tobacco all gone, when I gave her my pipe,
she sucked on it, saying, "This is not your old pipe!"

Then she asked where I was, and where I lived now.
She asked this in my dream, just as I tell it.
But I had to stay here. "I have to stay," I said,
"with my magistrate just a little while longer."
But it seemed to her, she said, I would never return.
Was I still laboring, a convict, at this place?
Was this why I had not yet returned to our plains?

I said to her I was no longer working.
"I have been teaching here, telling my stories
that others might know them, one day, from a book."
I was telling her this–that I told our stories
that the stories might live, not die with my death.
I talked, I then said I had been waiting to fetch her.
/Han≠kasso, I said, was soon coming to fetch her . . .

This was all in the dream, just as I tell it.
I dreamed all of this before I was woken.
I was lying there, then, startled and staring.
I could hear /A!kunta; sunlight was streaming.
/Har≠kasso had gone; my wife and son disappeared.
/A!kunta was outside, loudly milking a cow.

//Kabbo's Request for Thread

My thoughts spoke to me.
My thoughts, they spoke,
kept speaking in this manner,
commanding me to do this,
to speak to you, my mistress.

Thus my mouth, it speaks to you.
My mouth now says to you, a lady,
what I have long wished to say
when I lay thinking in the night,
while I lay awake upon my bed.

I thought that I would say to you,
I would come to ask my mistress, you,
if you would not give me thread
to sew in place the buttons
you gave me for my jacket.

Without this they will fall off.
Without thread, they will get lost.
And I–I keep on thinking of them,
I think, not a little gently, of the beauty
of these buttons that you gave me.

Return of the Moon

I

You know that I sit waiting for the moon,
for it to change for me, turn back for me,
that I might return, and soon, to the place once mine.
There I will hear the stories that we love to tell.
The plain's people, my people will be listening there
to the stories that come from far beyond the plains.
They listen to them, tell them, that I who have to wait
sitting in this sun, might hear them come to me—
these stories like the wind, coming through the air.
Already I feel them floating, while I await the moon,
because the sun grows colder now, the autumn is upon us.
And I know it, feel it, master, that I must soon return
to be there with my fellow-men, talking with my friends.

II

Master, you know how long I have sat waiting
that it might change for me, this moon turn back for me.
You know that here, living here, I work at women's work.
My fellow-men are those who can listen to the stories
that come to them from far-off, floating through the air.
Even now they hear them come from places far away,
these stories like the wind, floating like the winds.
But I am here, not there. Stories do not come to me
because I cannot visit—be there to hear them come.
These other servants—their place is not my place.
They do not know my stories, they do not know these words.
They go visiting their own kind; they are working people
who work at women's work. They are gardeners not hunters.

III

But the people of the plains—these are smoking people.
They go visiting each other's huts. They visit
to hear the stories; they sit there smoking, talking—
and the moon returns. And this is why I wait for it,
that I might set my feet upon the path, go back.
For I believe, and truly, I have only to await the moon

before I can tell my master, you, that it is now the time,
truly now the time for me to sit among my fellow-men—
people who still walk the plains, and go visiting their own kind.
For I always hear them listening, talking to each other;
I always dream of visiting, of sitting there among them.
For here I only work, and only with the women;
here I cannot talk to them; they only give me work.

IV

Therefore I must sit a little, first cooling my arms,
that the sitting might take a tiredness from them.
I must first listen, silent, waiting for the stories,
for those I long to hear to come floating to my ears.
I am listening for the road on which I travelled here.
For if one sits and waits, having once walked down a road,
the stories will come to you—they will follow after.
I can hear my three names—//Kabbo, Jantje, /Uh-ddoro
as I sit listening now: I think I hear them travelling.
For a story is the wind. A story is like the wind,
it comes floating through the air from a far-off place.
For our names are like the wind, and like the wind they float,
they come to people, floating, long before they see us.

V

Many mountains, high, might block a man's road home,
but his names can float behind, beyond the highest ranges.
His feet might walk the road, his names float through the air.
They go following a different path, floating far before him,
arriving where the others wait, already listening for him.
Then his kin know he's on his way—they hear his names returning.
I think I see him there already, I dream he has come home.
The trees grown tall, still taller, will be more beautiful to him.
He knows he was too long away; these are trees he knows.
I see him walking amongst those trees—I see him as I speak.

VI

The moon's return, its turning back, is all he waits for now.
He wants only that the moon might change, and soon,
to see again the waterholes where he once used to drink.
I think that he will set to work, re-building his old hut.
I dream I see him there, his family gathered to him.
His children will be with him, protecting his old waterholes,
guarding them from strangers who came while he was gone.
The waterholes his father owned, his father's father owned,
the waterholes his brother owned, which then passed to him;
these waters to which he brought !Kwaba-an, his wife,
that they should live there, married, not alone—
I think that there he will grow old, !Kwaba-an beside him.
I can see them living there, his children older, married,
his children's children talking, soon with understanding.

VII

Master, this is why I sit, waiting only for the Sundays
when I remain with you, and teach my stories to you.
I do not want another moon, for still one more to change.
I have told you of this one, and of my longing for it,
how I've waited for this moon's return, its turning back for me.
For many moons I have sat waiting, wishing for some boots,
boots strong enough for me to go, to walk the road back north.
For I will need such boots: the earth will soon be burning;
before I'm halfway there the sun will scorch the stones.
Indeed it is so long a road, so great a road I know
that I shall reach my place when trees are dry-leaved, dry,
when flowers along the roadside have long since died.

VIII

Then autumn will quickly be upon us on the plains.
In my place on the plains, autumn will come over us.
Once more the moon will turn, but I will see it, changed:
I will not await its falling off, watch for its turning back.
There I will have the gun that you have promised me;
I will no longer starve, nor need to steal a sheep.

In the middle of the cold, a gun takes care of an old man;
it will kill a springbok, even in strong wind, strong cold.
The moon might change, turn back, but I will not set out.
I will be there at the place whose name my master knows.
I will remain, then, at the place you have written down.
There it is, you know it, having placed it in your book;
it is there already, in the book, my name //Kabbo there beside it.

Index of Poems by Narrator

Notes to the Poems

The phonetic symbols //, !, /, and ≠, represent the various clicks in the /Xam language. I have retained them for the visually estranging effect they create, as a reminder of the 'foreignness' of the world of the /Xam. If they were actually pronounced, they would in most cases disturb the rhythm or metre of the poems.

THE RAIN-SORCERER: The practice of shamanism (or sorcery) was central to the /Xam, informing many aspects of their life at the deepest level. The practices of the shaman (or sorcerer) provided a supernatural technology intended to overcome the limits of nature. Whereas we today tend to believe in the magic of technology, the /Xam believed in a technology of magic. In the trance dance–a regular, unifying rite in any clan–the shaman would make contact with the spirit-world and there tap a source of power (called !gi) which would enable him or her to engage in such diverse tasks as healing the sick, making rain, controlling the movements of game, and going on out-of-body travel to ascertain how people in other camps were faring.

PRAYER TO THE NEW MOON: This prayer precedes the mythical account (of which there are eight versions in the Bleek collection) of the origins of death. Common to all of them is the moon's pronouncement that he, Moon, will die but live again (as he waxes and wanes), while the Hare will be punished for distorting this message. Mathias Guenther notes in his *Bushman Folktales* (1989) that "in neither the /Xam nor the Nharo case is there any evidence that the moon was regarded as the bringer of rain, game and food, let alone the object of worship. Both have been tenacious stereotype ideas of westerners about Bushman supernaturalism." (p. 82)

THE SOUND OF THE STARS: For the /Xam, as for many other supposedly 'primitive' peoples, the predominant categories used to make sense of the universe were drawn from the living world. This is something so remote from modern understanding that we need to remind ourselves that there actually was a time before men and women discovered the existence of truly inanimate, 'dead' matter. Earth, wind, water, and stars were anything but instances of 'mere matter.' Indeed, it could probably never have occurred to the /Xam that life might be a side issue in the universe and not its pervading rule.

THROWING FIRE AT THE STARS: In /Xam ceremonies, Dorothea Bleek has written, "certain stars are asked for certain foods." Thus Canopus and Sirius were invoked in the belief that they would bring success in the search for 'Bushmen's rice' (ants' chrysalides). It is the custom of Bleek and Lloyd to give the western names for stars or constellations in their collection, and I have followed them in this.

THE GIRL WHO CREATED THE MILKY WAY: Many of the /Xam narratives deal with people of the "first" or "Early Race." This imagined primal time, before the /Xam themselves came into existence, was regarded as formative in many ways. It was then that the natural, social and cosmological orders were established. And yet these various orders are also shown to be precarious. This particular story of a maiden violating menstrual taboos while in her menstrual hut is a case in point. "Unless girls observe menarcheal proscriptions," writes Mathias Guenther in his *Bushman Folktales*, "not only is the moral integrity of the society as a whole in jeopardy, but the very ontological state of man and the cultural domain he has created is threatened with anarchy." (p. 36) Even so, stories like "The Girl Who Created the Milky Way" were not just cautionary tales. Many of them emphasize the courage, creativity, and magical power of women. While the latter could be dangerous, causing the reversal of humans into primal animals, they were also responsible, as several myths affirm, for tending and obtaining Fire and, not least, for the creation of galaxies like the Milky Way.

THE SUN, THE MOON, AND THE KNIFE: For the /Xam, the relationship between sun and moon was one of unceasing antagonism. Both were usually considered to be men, though the gender of the moon was also thought to change according to its different phases, becoming female when full, male when new once more.

WHAT HAPPENS WHEN YOU DIE: The /Xam believed that everyone had a "wind" associated with him or her, and that when they died this "wind" would blow, removing their footprints from the earth. It was also believed that the cavity in any new moon was the "catching place" for people who had recently died.

THE NATURE OF /KAGGEN: This extract is constructed around an incident in which the /Xam trickster called /Kaggen (also known as Mantis), the favorite hero of their folklore, meets with one of his frequent trials, only to escape and prove his supernatural powers once

62

more. /Kaggen is a figure that not only represents all that is beyond the human order—the wild, the natural, the animal—but also possesses a nature based on often violent contraries. Indeed, as Guenther has written, "ambiguity" is the quality at the core of this mythical being. "It is exemplified in many ways. Trickster is at one time human or animal, at another animal, or tree or plant; he is both vindictive and destructive and beneficent and creative; cunning and readily duped. What he delights in doing, whatever his state and disposition, is to play tricks on other beings." (p. 115) Here, as is evident, one of his pranks has backfired—something that is all too common. But it serves to demonstrate his extraordinary powers of creativity and recuperation in the midst of calamity.

THE DAWN'S HEART STAR: TWO FRAGMENTS: The Dawn's Heart Star is a sidereal and animal narrative many pages in length. It is probably the most striking of the myth cycles in the Bleek and Lloyd collection, dealing, among much else, with the relations between the Dawn's Heart Star (the planet Jupiter, thought, like other stars, to have numbered among the people of the "Early Race") and his wife, the Lynx.

BLUE MIST LIKE SMOKE: The /Xam word "!kho" literally means "a blue mist which resembles smoke."

THE ORIGIN OF THE MOON: This is the culminating extract from the myth which deals with the Mantis's creation of the Eland. There is a useful summary of the symbolism of the story in Patricia Vinnicombe's study of Drakensberg rock art, *People of the Eland* (1976), and a more extended analysis in Roger L. Hewitt's *Structure, Meaning and Ritual in the Narratives of the Southern San* (1986).

A FEATHER THROWN INTO THE SKY: The /Xam commonly referred to the waning of the moon as its "falling away" or "falling off."

THE MAIDEN AND THE RAIN: In a summary of Bushman mythology in his *Bushman Folktales*, Guenther writes: "Creation, according to Bushman myth, occurred twice, leaving two orders of existence, primal time and the new order. The first order of creation contained some basic flaws: the primal humans and animals and animal-humans behaved 'without customs': violating in particular the norms and mores pertaining to eating, sharing, marriage, proper kin relations and menarcheal proscriptions. Just as the social and moral condition of the 'early' race was not firmly fixed, so also was their ontological state precarious and replete with ambiguity. . . . The ambiguity of the early humans ... became manifested primarily when a young woman violated her menstrual taboos and thereby brought about her own and her band members' transformation into frogs or other animals, or even trees or stones. The human, social and cultural orders were thus capable of instantaneous reversal back to animal and nature." (p. 35)

CATCHING A PORCUPINE: It would be wrong to assume (as it is, perhaps, very easy to do) that the /Xam lived in a world of total supernaturalism, surrounded by nothing but spirit figures and other fantastical creatures from primal time. The Bleek and Lloyd collection also includes a large store of zoological and botanical knowledge which supplements the type of knowledge to be found in /Xam mythology. Thus one finds several extracts like "Catching a Porcupine" which give details of some of the hunting lore passed on from one generation to the next. In this particular case, the narrative has an obviously didactic function.

SNEEZING OUT A LION: The /Xam believed that many illnesses were caused by an animal entering the body of the afflicted person. This could be an owl, a lion, a springbok–even a butterfly. In curing the person, the sorcerer or shaman would work to expel the animal from the person it had entered, imitating the particular call or cry of the animal at the moment of expulsion. He or she was aided in this by the use of buchu (an aromatic herb derived from any of the several species of Rutaceæ), usually given by the patient's family.

SORCERERS ARE LIKE LIONS: In the /Xam mind, lions were often associated with harm, disease, and general malevolence. Sorcerers or shamans, who could work for evil as well as good, were often said to go about their sorcery in the guise of a lion. Those whose influence was malignant were known to be particularly hostile towards good-looking people. In the context of this poem, it is important to know that the failure of a cure was often explained in terms of a malignant sorcerer firing invisible arrows at the sick person, sometimes under the very noses of the people attempting to heal him or her.

THE POWERS OF THE DEAD: According to the /Xam, as Patricia Vinnicombe has written, "the thinking powers of man, or literally 'thinking strings', were to be found in the sides of their throats; a belief possibly originating from an awareness of the jugular pulse during moments of stress, tension or intense concentration." (p. 260)

These "thinking strings" also referred to the /Xam concept of consciousness. Theirs was a society, as Vinnicombe also writes, "where ultimate unity depended on its orientation towards an invisible power." (p. 352) The consciousness of these channels of invisible force was also described as "thinking strings" by the Bushmen.

THE LOST TOBACCO POUCH: A SONG: Many commentators have mentioned the Bushman fondness for tobacco. They "adore smoking" wrote Dorothea Bleek and A.M. Duggin-Cronin in their *The Bushman Tribes of Southern Africa* (1942): "Everyone smokes, even the children." //Kabbo himself specifically calls the /Xam a "smoking people."

THE STORY OF RUYTER: The word "riem" in the first stanza of this poem is the Afrikaans word for a leather thong or rope often used as a bridle or harness.

SONG OF THE BROKEN STRING: There must have come an actual point in time when certain members of the /Xam were forced to realize something almost inconceivable: namely, that their own culture was coming to an end; that for them there was no future. A realization of this order is implicit in the lament composed by Xaa-ttin in memory of the sorcerer !Huin T Kui-ten. It makes for what is probably the most powerful single record of /Xam life losing its coherence under the impact of other encroaching cultures. The "people" referred to here are, presumably, the European settler population.

XAA-TTIN'S LAMENT: In the penultimate chapter of *People of the Eland*, Vinnicombe writes of a "renowned sorcerer who was mortally wounded by a Boer commando" and who "passed on what information he could to a young Bushman [Xaa-ttin] selected to inherit the secrets of rain-making. The rites included a song described as a 'string' which called the rain-bull, but because of increasingly unsettled circumstances, the chosen man apparently never practiced his art." (p. 344) In this piece the narrator, Dia!kwain, speaks of his father, Xaa-ttin, who in turn refers to the dead sorcerer, !Huin T. Kui-ten. Xaa-ttin's song may be read not only as the guilt-stricken lament of a man who has not been able to carry on one of the most important of his people's rites, but also as a sign of the end of the /Xam way of life, and therefore of the /Xam as a whole. Perhaps the closest analogy to it in English literature is that poetry of the nineteenth century whose tone of inconsolable longing registers the effects of a dying faith, specifically the death of the Christian God.

//KABBO'S ROAD INTO CAPTIVITY: From the surviving prison records, we know that //Kabbo was found guilty on two counts of "R.S. Goods"—presumably receiving stolen goods. It seems that he was arrested for sheep stealing. Louis Anthing's official report of 1863 does much to explain why so many /Xam resorted to stock-theft, giving as it does the essential background to a narrative like this one: "in consequence of the colonists having guns and horses, and their being expert hunters (the pursuit of game being their daily occupation), the wild game of the country has become scarce, and almost inaccessible to the Bushmen, whose weapon is the bow and arrow, having a comparatively short range." Anthing went on to note that "ostrich eggs, honey, grass-seed, and roots had all become exceedingly scarce, the ostriches being destroyed by hunters, the seed and roots in consequence of the intrusion of the colonists' flocks. From these various causes, the Bushman's subsistence failed him, and in many cases they died of hunger." (*Cape Parliamentary Papers*: Report A 39, 1863, p.4)

THE NAME OF MY PLACE: This encounter presumably took place while //Kabbo was travelling by train in the Cape Town vicinity. His use of the word "Bitterpits" (alternatively "Bitterputs") to name his place of origin is one indication among many in the Bleek and Lloyd collection of his degree of familiarity with the European settler society, and of the degree to which he had already been acculturated.

//KABBO TELLS ME HIS DREAM: Apparently, //Kabbo's wife, !Kwaba-an, was to have joined him while he was still living with the Bleeks in Mowbray. For reasons which remain unclear, this never materialized. It seems that his only company must have been that of the much younger informant, /A!kunta, who also lived with the Bleeks for a period in the early 1870s. In her introduction to *Specimens of Bushmen Folklore* (1911), Lucy Lloyd remarks that //Kabbo "much enjoyed the thought that the Bushman stories would become known by means of books." (p. x) It is evident that what he refers to as "teaching" here—namely, the narration of /Xam stories and lore—was of considerable importance, even pride, to him. Like Bleek and Lloyd, //Kabbo was probably aware that his stories might soon be lost forever.

RETURN OF THE MOON: Among the most powerful of the autobiographical narratives in the Bleek and Lloyd collection, "The Return of the Moon" is more than a record of one man's acute homesickness. It also sounds and even anticipates that note of exile which is to become pervasive in much South African literature in the twentieth century. At the same time, it confirms the importance of stories and story-telling in the social life of the /Xam and provides incidental information about the inheritance of waterholes. Although W. H. Bleek noted in an official report of 1875 that //Kabbo could be induced to remain in Mowbray "only by the promise of a greatly longed for reward" (his sentence ended soon after he went to live with the Bleeks and he remained there for almost two more years), we have no way of knowing whether he ever received or was able to make use of the gun Bleek promised to send him. What we do know is that he died within a year or so of his return to "Bitterpits," his place on the plains in the Kenhardt district of the northwestern Cape.

Appendix

Some examples of original transcripts from the Bleek and Lloyd Collection

Note: these are given here under the titles which Bleek and Lloyd gave the extracts, not those which I have used for my versions.

1. SUN, MOON, AND STARS. The sun is down, it comes out of the mountain, it stands above in the heaven, the sun goes in the heaven. The moon comes out of the mountain, it goes in the heaven; the star comes out of the mountain; it mounts the heaven. Many stars are in heaven. The star woman, the star mother leads star child, it runs out. The man star comes running, he also brings (leads) the star child, he mounts running, the star mother brings the star child, he runs away, he runs into the clouds.

2. /KAUNU, A RAINMAKER. /Kaunu he used to strike the bowstring, and the clouds came out, while we others slept; and the people awoke while the clouds had shut in the place while the people were sleeping. And the people awoke when the clouds had shut out the sun.

And the rain made a cloak (of rain), it rained there, poured down while the sun set. Day broke while it rained there, and the sun again the sun set and the rain in the ... the rain broke. And it altogether broke while it did not again rain. We were sleeping; he sat taking up the bow, while we were sleeping. And we ... we heard the bow-string as he was striking it there.

3. THE STORY OF RUYTER. Ruyter was brought up by white men, he died while he was with white men. The Boer has been beating him about herding the sheep that he had not herded the sheep well, therefore the Boer was beating him with the strap which the people tie under the oxen's necks, that strap it was with which the Boer had bound him upon the wagon, the Boer beat him, as he lay bound on the wagon and when the Boers intended to stop beating him, a Boer unloosed him, he did this when the Boer was unloosening him, he fainted. People were those who came to lift him because the Boer had beaten him to death. He told the other people about it that the other people seemed to think he did not feel pain that it felt as if the Boer had beaten him to death. It did not seem as if he would live. He had looked after the sheep he told the people that it felt as if he should not be long where he was because of the pain which he felt in his

body. He it was who told the other people that the middle of his body ached badly, he was the one who walked although he ached where his body felt like that for the Boer not only beat him but when the Boer was beating him he trampled on him while he was beating him. Therefore he felt that it seemed as if the Boer had trampled breaking his body's middle. This happened that beating was the one he died of.

4. SONG OF THE BROKEN STRING. The people were those who broke (took hold of and broke) for me the string/thong. Therefore, the place became/was like this to me on account of it, because the string/thong was that which had broken for me. Therefore, the place (country) does not feel to me as the place (country) used to feel to me, on account of it. For the place (country) feels as if it stood open (empty?)/felt to stand open before me because the string/thong has/was broken for me. Therefore, the place (country) does/did not feel pleasant to me on account of it.

5. //KABBO IN THE TRAIN. We have not heard, I have said to thee that the train (fire wagon) is nice. I sat nicely in the train, we two sat in it, we, I and the black man. A woman seized my arm, she drew me inside because I would have fallen. She drew me in. I sat opposite to the black man. His face was black, his mouth was also black, for they were black. White men are those whose faces were (are) red: for it is that they are handsome. The black man is ugly. For it is that his mouth is black. For it is that his face is black truly. The black man then asked me, "Where doest thou come from?" I said to the black man, I come from this place (home). The black man then asked me, "What is the name?" I said to the black man, "My place is Bitterpits."

6. ABOUT CATCHING/WAITING FOR A PORCUPINE. Father was used to say to me that I should, if I were sitting waiting for a porcupine that I the time which the Milky Way turns back upon it, it is the one which I know that the time which the porcupine returns upon it, now is.

Father taught me about the stars; that I should if I were sitting waiting by a porcupine's hole, I must watch the stars, the place where the stars fall (at) it is the one which I must greatly watch. For this place it really is that which the porcupine is at; that which the stars fall at.

I must also feel the wind. The things which I must watch them as my father thus spoke; he taught me about them, the thing which I must watch them.

Father said to me about it, that I should watch the wind; for the porcupine is not a thing which will return coming out of the wind. For he is used to returning to come across the wind in a slanting direction while he feels that he wishes he might smell. Therefore, he is used to go across the wind in a slanting direction on account of it; while he feels that he wishes that he might smell for his nostril are those which tell him about it that harm is at this place/these places.

Father used to say to me that I should not breathe strongly if I were sitting waiting for a porcupine for, a thing which does not a little hear, it is. I also must not rustle strongly for a porcupine is a thing which has a fine sense of hearing/does not hear a little, it is.

Therefore we are used, sitting gently to turn around on account of it, while we feel that we fear if we were to/should have done so as he came he would have heard.

7. RAIN WASHED OUT A DEAD MAN'S FOOTSTEPS. A person who rains (a person who dies he is) the rain falls, taking away his footsteps so that his footsteps may no longer be there. The rain presently falling takes away his footsteps, when we have just put him in the ground (to his grave). When we have just put him into the grave, and we are filling in the earth, the rain falls while we have not yet covered it (over with bushes). And the rain falls and we afterwards we cover (it with bushes) cover it, laying the bushes upon the earth while we intend to heap in stones, heap, laying stones upon the bushes, in order that the bushes may also not be bare. Therefore we heap on stones shutting in the bushes.

8. THE MANTIS AND THE MOON. The mantis formerly when he had piercing broken the gall, the gall broke over his head, and his eyes were closed. It was like night. And he thus, he crawled along, he felt with his hands he felt with his hands that place along which he was crawling. And he, feeling with his hands reached the bare place, feeling with his hands, reached the ostrich's bare place. He feeling with his hands, discovered an old feather, he lifted it up, he lifted it up, he drew it across his lips (wetting it). He wiped his eyes (with it).

And, he threw it up he exclaimed, "Thou shalt stick fast along/to the sky; thou shalt become the moon, thou art the one who must be shining. The sun is the one who must set, thou who art the moon, thou art the one who must be shining at night. Thou are the one who is shining (must) lift up the darkness from the people. The sun is the one who rises/who must rise, and the people head the game on account of it. Thou art the one who must shine/be shining when the sun has set at night."

9. //KABBO ASKING ME FOR THREAD TO SEW ON HIS BUTTONS THAT I GAVE HIM. My thoughts spoke to me, my thoughts (in this manner) they spoke to me, therefore my mouth speaks to thee, my mouth thus, my mouth says to the lady that which I should speak to thee I thus thought in the night while I lay; I thinking lay; lay upon the bed. I thought that I would say to thee that thou shouldst give me thread, I should sew, sewing in place the buttons on the jacket, the buttons which, thou didst give them to me for they would be falling down for me upon the ground; for, I not a little gently think of them; for they are handsome.

10. SNEEZING. I think that /Han≠kasso has seen !Kwaba-an, and has seen Swaba-//ken. I think that !Kwaba-an calls my name; I think that Swaba-//ken calls my name; I think that //Goa-ka-!kwi calls my name, he asks Kerru about me. He asks Kerru, "Where is //Kabbo?" Kerru answers, "(Your) father is with his master." His (the son's) mother asks him, he says to his mother, "(Your) husband has stayed with his master."

This is what I think, I believe that /Han≠kasso has seen Swaba-//ken; I think that she has called my name, because I sneeze. I think that my wife called my name because I sneeze. I think that my son calls my name, I think that my daughter calls my name, I think so, because I sneeze.

I think that my daughter's husband says to my daughter: "These are father's trousers which his master gave him telling him to give them to me." That is what I think. Her mother asks, "Are those father's trousers?" Her daughter's husband says to her, "They are (your) husband's trousers which he gave me." I think so because I sneeze.

My wife asks him, "Are those (your) father-in-law's trousers?" She says to her daughter-in-law, "Husband seems to want me to come and talk to him, for he is staying with his master; I think he is telling me that his son has been staying with me, we will go to him." I think so, for I sneeze.

11. //KABBO THINKING OF GOING HOME. Thou knowest that I sit waiting for the moon to turn back for me, that I may return to my place. That I may listen to all the people's stories that which they tell; they listen to the Flat Bushmen's stories from the other side of the place. They are those which they thus tell, they are listening to them; while the other !Xoe-ssho!-kui (the sun) becomes a little warm, that I

may sit in the sun; that I may sitting, listen to the stories which yonder come which are the stories which come from a distance. Then, I shall get hold of a story from them, because the sun feels a little warm; while I feel that I must altogether visit; that I may be talking with them, my fellow men.

For I do work here, at women's household work. My fellow men are those who are listening to stories from afar, which float along; they are listening to stories from other places. For I am here; I do not obtain stories; because I do not visit, so that I might hear stories which float along; while I feel that the people of another place are here; they do not possess my stories. They do not talk my language; for they visit their like; while they feel that work's people (they) are, those who work keeping houses in order. They work (at) food; that the food may grow for them; that they should get food which is good, that which is new food.

The Flat Bushmen go to each other's huts; that they may smoking sit in front of them. Therefore, they obtain stories at them; because they are used to visit; for smoking's people they are. As regards myself (?) I am waiting that the moon may turn back for me; that I may set my feet forward in the path. For, I verily (?) think that I must only await the moon; that I may tell my Master, that I feel this is the time when I should sit among my fellow men, who walking meet their like. They are listening to them; for, I do not think of visits; (that) I out to visit; (that) I ought to talk with my fellow men; for, I work here, together with women; and I do not talk with them; for they merely send me to work.

I must first sit a little, cooling my arms; that the fatigue may go out to them; because I sit. I do merely listen, watching for a story, which I want to hear; while I sit waiting for it; that it may float into my ear. These are those to which I am listening with all my ears; while I feel that I sit silent. I must wait (listening) behind me, while I listen along the road; they (my three names) [Jantje, /Uh-ddoro, and //Kabbo] float along to my place; I will turn backwards (with my ears) to my feet's heels, on which I went; while I feel that a story is the wind. It (the story) is wont to float along to another place. Then our names do pass through those people; while they do not perceive our bodies go along. For, our names are those which, floating, reach a different place. The mountains lie between (the two different roads). A man's name passes behind the mountain's back; those (names) with which he returning goes along. While he (the man) feels that the road is that which lies thus; and the man is upon it. The road is around his place, because the road curves. The people who dwell at another place, their ear does listening go to meet the returning man's names; those with which he returns. He will examine the place. For, the trees of the place seem to be handsome; Because they have grown tall; while the man of the place (//Kabbo) has not seen them, that he might walk among them. For, he came to live at a different place; his place it is not. For, it was so with him that people were those who brought him to the people's place, that he should first come to work for a little while at it. He is the one who thinks of (his) place, that he must be the one to return.

He only awaits the return of the moon; that the moon may go round, that he may return (home) that he may examine the water pits; those at which he drank. He will work, putting the old hut in order, while he feels that he has gathered his children together, that they may work, putting the water in order for him; for, he did go away, leaving the place, while the strangers were those who walked at the place. Their place it is not; for //Kabbo's father's father's place it was. And then//Kabbo's father did possess it; when //Kabbo's father's father died, //Kabbo's father was the one who possessed it. And when //Kabbo's father died, //Kabbo's eldest brother was the one who possessed the place; //Kabbo's eider brother died, (then) //Kabbo possessed the place. And then //Kabbo married when grown up, bringing !Kwaba-an to the place, because he felt that he was alone; therefore, he grew old with his wife at the place, while he felt that his children were married. His children's children talked, they felt that they talked with understanding....*

Therefore, I must sit waiting for the Sundays on which I remain here, on which I continue to teach thee. I do not again await another moon, for this moon is the one about which I told thee. Therefore, I desired that it should do thus, that it should return for me. For I have sat waiting for the boots, that I must putting on go in them. Those which are strong for the road. For the sun will go along, burning strongly. And then the earth becomes hot, while I am still going along halfway. I must go together with the warm sun, while the ground is hot. For a little road it is not, the one which is here. For a great road it is, it is long. I should reach my place when the trees are dry. For, I shall walk, letting the flowers become dry while I still follow the path.

Then, autumn will quickly be (upon) us there; when I am sitting at my (own) place. For, I shall not go to other places; for I must remain at my (own) place, the name of which I had told my Master; he knows it; he knows, (having) put it down. And thus my name is plain (beside) it. It is there that I sit waiting for the gun; and then, he will send the gun to me there; while he sends the gun in a cart; that which running, takes me the gun. While he thinks that I have not forgotten; that my body may be quiet, as it was when I was with him; while I feel than I shoot, feeding myself. For starvation was that which I was bound on account of it, for starvation's food, that hunger which I starving turned back from following the sheep on account of it. Therefore I, I lived with him, that I might get a gun from him; that I might possess it. That I might myself shoot, feeding myself, while I do not eat my companions' food. For I eat my own game.

For a gun is that which takes care of an old man; it is that with which we kill the springbok which go through the cold (wind). We do, satisfied with food, lie down (in our huts) in the cold (wind). The gun, is the one which is strong in the wind. It getting, satisfies a man's hunger (in the middle of the cold).

*At this point in his narration, //Kabbo embarks upon a digression several pages in length. For reasons of space, I have not included this. (SW)